THE TRIAL

Kafka's Unholy Trinity

TWAYNE'S MASTERWORK STUDIES

Robert Lecker, General Editor

THE TRIAL

Kafka's Unholy Trinity

Henry Sussman

TWAYNE PUBLISHERS • NEW YORK
Maxwell Macmillan Canada • Toronto
Maxwell Macmillan International • New York Oxford Singapore Sydney

Twayne's Masterwork Studies No. 107

The Trial: Kafka's Unholy Trinity
Henry Sussman

Twayne Publishers   Maxwell Macmillan Canada, Inc.
Macmillan Publishing Company   1200 Eglinton Avenue East
866 Third Avenue   Suite 200
New York, New York 10022   Don Mills, Ontario M3C 3N1

Library of Congress Cataloging-in-Publication Data
Sussman, Henry.
    The trial: Kafka's unholy trinity/Henry Sussman.
        p   cm.—(Twayne's masterwork studies; no. 107)
    Includes bibliographical references and index.
    ISBN 0–8057–9408–5 (hc: alk. paper). — ISBN 0–8057–8577–9 (pb: alk.
paper)
        1. Kafka, Franz, 1883–1924. Prozess. I. Title. II. Series.
PT2621.A26P776   1993   92–43021
833'.912—dc20   CIP

The paper used in this publication meets the minimum requirements of American
National Standard for Information Sciences—Permanence of Paper for Printed Library
Materials. ANSI Z3948-1984. ∞ ™

10 9 8 7 6 5 4 3 2 1   (hc)
10 9 8 7 6 5 4 3 2 1   (pb)

Printed in the United States of America

Contents

Note on the References and Acknowledgments　　　　　　　　　*vii*
Chronology: Franz Kafka's Life and Works　　　　　　　　　　*ix*

LITERARY AND HISTORICAL CONTEXT
    1. The History of an Image　　　　　　　　　　　　　3
    2. At the Crossroads of the Twentieth Century　　　10
    3. The Trial of Interpretation and Its Critical
        Reception　　　　　　　　　　　　　　　　19

A READING
    4. Rehearsals　　　　　　　　　　　　　　　　35
    5. A Courthouse of Codes and Messages　　　　63
    6. Bearings　　　　　　　　　　　　　　　　　95
    7. The Society of Withdrawal　　　　　　　　112
    8. The Parable of Parables　　　　　　　　　135

Notes and References　　　　　　　　　　　　　　　*151*
Bibliography　　　　　　　　　　　　　　　　　　*158*
Index　　　　　　　　　　　　　　　　　　　　*167*

Franz Kafka, about 1920
© *Archiv Klaus Wagenbach*

Note on the References and Acknowledgments

I have drawn inspiration from the late pioneering Kafka critic Roman Karst in two ways: first, from his intrepid dedication to his subject and all conceptual issues related to it; and second, from his outstanding Kafka library, which owing to the generosity of Dr. Bronia Karst of Buffalo, furnished me with much of the secondary material I incorporated into the present volume.

As I indicate in chapter 3, Professor Richard Jayne of the University of Göttingen, Germany, gave me invaluable assistance by suggesting which recent contributions to the secondary literature needed to be incorporated into my overview and the bibliography. I am indebted not only to his knowledge of the Kafka literature, but also to his camaraderie in our shared enterprise of expanding interest in Kafka. Professor Jayne's much too early death in late 1991 constituted a major loss for Kafka scholarship.

Ruth Starkman, an advanced student in the Program in Comparative Literature, wrote the chronology. Jan Plug, Anna Schatz, and Michele Sharp, also in the Program, furnished indispensable editorial assistance.

The writing and assembly of this study in the spring of 1990 were made possible by a residence fellowship at the Camargo Foundation, Cassis, France, so ably maintained and improved by Michael Pretina and the late Jean-François Gagneux; and also by a sabbatical leave from the State University of New York at Buffalo.

Mrs. Diane Forrest and Ms. Elizabeth Parker, staff members in the Program in Comparative Literature at SUNY/Buffalo, rendered enormous service to me by transforming my barely legible notebooks into clean, readable text.

I am much indebted to the general editor of this series, Robert Lecker, for his painstaking and careful editing, and to the editorial staff of Twayne Publishers for their generous and always productive assistance.

All references in this book are to the Definitive Editions published by Schocken Books. The photograph of Franz Kafka appears with the kind permission of Mr. Klaus Wagenbach, Berlin; original line drawings from *The Trial* are reprinted with the permission of Schocken Books and Martin Secker and Warburg.

In this study, I have enlarged upon earlier work by incorporating the inter "personal" level of Joseph K.'s interactions and "awareness" into the allegory of textual production and interpretation I have elsewhere explored. Where my formulations have not improved since my 1977 article in *PMLA*, "The Court as Text: Inversion, Supplanting, and Derangement in Kafka's *Der Prozeß*," I have simply appropriated them, to the tune of two or three pages. I am grateful to the editors of *PMLA* for this possibility.

If this introduction to *The Trial* in any way arouses readers' interest in the novel and other of Kafka's works and clarifies their apprehension of its events, it will have more than succeeded in its purpose.

Chronology:
Franz Kafka's Life and Works

<u>1883</u>	Franz Kafka, named after Franz Josef, emperor of Austria- *when?* Hungary, born 3 July, to Hermann Kafka, the owner of a small street-front shop selling inexpensive women's wear and notions, and Julie Löwy. Hermann was the son of a Kosher butcher in Osek.
1886–1892	Two brothers, Georg (1885–87) and Heinrich (1887–88) are born and die. Births of three sisters: Gabriele (Elli, 1889), Valerie (Valli, 1890), and Ottilie (Ottla, 1892)—all of whom would die as a result of Hitler's "Final Solution."
1889	Begins attending Deutsche Knabenschule (German primary school for boys) in Prague.
1893–1901	Attends highly competitive, but second-best German high school, the Altstädter Gymnasium in Prague. Receives classical humanistic education; scores above average in Latin, Greek, religion, German, geography, history, and natural sciences, but has trouble with math.
1896	Bar Mitvahed.
1901	Graduates from the gymnasium. Vacations on the North Sea islands. Begins classes in September at Prague's Charles-Ferdinand University, where he studies law.
1903	Takes state exams in history of the law. Stays at Dr. Lahmann's sanatorium near Dresden. Shows early writings, now lost, to friend Oskar Pollak.
1905	Health begins to deteriorate; spends four weeks at Zuckmantel Sanatorium in Silesia. Has affair with an older woman. Takes exams in Austrian civil law.

1906   Takes exams in political and international law. In April starts work in law offices of Dr. Richard Löwy. In June takes exams in Roman and German law. Submits doctoral thesis entitled *German and Austrian State Law: Common Law and Political Economy.* Qualifies for doctorate in law 18 June.

1907   Vacations in Triesch where he begins relationship with Viennese student Hedwig Weiler. Assumes temporary post at the Assicurazioni Generali insurance company in anticipation of Hedwig's relocation to Prague, although she never carries plan through. Writes "Wedding Preparations in the Country."

1908   Publishes eight prose pieces under the title "Betrachung" (Meditation) in the bimonthly *Hyperion.* Begins as junior assistant at the Workers' Accident Insurance Institute for the Kingdom of Bohemia. Establishes close friendship with Max Brod. Frequents coffeehouses, cabarets, and brothels.

1909   Ten-day holiday with Max and Otto Brod to Riva on Lake Garda. Sees flying competition in Brescia; in September the daily newspaper *Bohemia* publishes Kafka's "Die Aeroplane in Brescia," the first description of airplanes to appear in German newsprint. Makes numerous business trips. In May *Hyperion* publishes "Conversations with the Suppliant" and excerpts from "Description of a Struggle."

1911   Friendship with Yiddish actor Yitzak Löwy, who inspires Kafka's interest in Judaism. Makes business trips to Reichenberg and Friedland. Meets industrialist and natural-health practitioner Moritz Schnitzer, who proposes vegetarian cures, sunbathing, and natural healing; this approach to health influences Kafka's understanding of medicine for years to come.

1912   Writes first draft of *Amerika* in May. Spends summer with Brod on trip to Goethe Museum in Weimar. Meets Ernst Rowohlt and Kurt Wolff. Attends lectures on Palestine and America. Contemplates suicide in October when family insists he take over the asbestos factory. Writes "The Judgment" and a draft of "The Stoker." Writes "The Metamorphosis." Meets Felice Bauer. "Meditation" published by Rowohlt.

1913   Promoted to vice-secretary of institute. "The Stoker" published by Kurt Wolff in May. "The Judgment" published in June. Proposes marriage to Felice; she accepts. Meets Ernst Weiss. Attends "Second International Congress for First Aid and Accident Prevention" in Vienna. From Vienna continues trip through Trieste, Venice, Verona, and Desenzeno to Dr. von Hartanger's sanatorium, where he has an affair with an 18-year-old Swiss girl. Meets Grete Bloch, the 21-year-old friend of Felice, who comes to Prague as Felice's messenger, begins mediation between Felice and Kafka, and develops intimate correspondence with Kafka. Bloch later claims to have had a son by Kafka, unknown to him, conceived ca. summer 1915.

1914 Begins writing "In the Penal Colony." Tuberculosis in general population.

1915 Wins Theodor Fontane Prize, including gift of 800 marks. "Before the Law" published by Kurt Wolff in December. "The Metamorphosis" appears in *Die weissen Blätter* in October and in book form in November.

1917 In January suffers from stomach trouble and insomnia. Felice comes to Prague in July and they become engaged again. Travels with Felice to Arad, Hungary, to visit her sister Else Braun. Travels to Budapest alone and sees Yiddish actor Yitzak Löwy. In August has lung hemorrhage and is diagnosed as tubercular. Takes three-month sick leave; joins sister Ottla in Zürau. Publishes "Jackals and Arabs" and "A Report from an Academy" in *Der Jude*.

1918 Leaves Zürau in April in relatively good health. Resumes work at institute. Spends summer gardening at Troja. Takes two-week precautionary vacation to Turov in September; diseased lung is no worse. Upon return in October, succumbs to a flu, which would eventually claim 20 million lives in Europe. Remains ill for six weeks. Awarded Austrian Decoration for developing worker's program at Frankenstein.

1919 Returns to Schelesen, Czechoslovakia, and meets Julie Wohryzek, daughter of a Czech-Jewish shoemaker and syna-gogue custodian. Proposes marriage, and becomes engaged to Julie; Hermann Kafka objects and threatens to emigrate if marriage carried through. The collection *In the Penal Colony* is published. Returns to Schelesen again in November and writes *Letter to His Father*. Returns to Prague and to work. Recurrent illness.

1920 Promoted to institute secretary. Begins writing *Er (He)*. Continuous ill health since flu. Takes leave to Meran. Corresponds with Milena Jesenska-Pollak, his Czech translator and Viennese writer, rebellious daughter of prominent Czech family, wife of Ernst Pollak, German-Jewish writer. Spends

June and July in Vienna, including four days with Milena. In July breaks engagement with Julie. Goes to Gmund with Milena, who says she cannot leave her husband. *A Country Doctor* published. Anti-Jewish riots in November. Health worsens; suffers fevers and shortness of breath.

1921   Stays in Matliary; suffers many minor illnesses, but lung no worse. Meets Robert Klopstock, 21-year-old medical student from Budapest, who makes himself Kafka's official attendant. Tries to break with Milena. Returns to work at institute in August. Suffering coughing and has trouble breathing. Meets Milena in Prague in September–October and gives her diaries; tells her Brod has seen them, and requests that they be burned after his death. Begins new diary in October. Writes "First Sorrow."

1922   Spends January and February in Spindelmühle, Silesia. Writes "A Hunger Artist." Begins writing *The Castle*. Receives promotion to first vice-secretary. Writes "Investigations of a Dog." Applies for temporary retirement in July (has not worked since October 1921); the institute grants him a pension and requests regular certificate of proof that he is still alive. Stays during June and July with sister Ottla in Plana 60 miles south of Prague. "A Hunger Artist" published in October by the monthly *Die Neue Rundschau*. Costly treatments for his illness are causing financial problems.

1923   Suffers ear and stomach aches, insomnia. Spends most of the winter in bed. Resumes Hebrew studies, this time with 19-year-old Puah Bentovim, who, unlike Kafka's previous teachers, speaks and teaches modern Hebrew. Receives visit from Hugo Bermann, who suggests Kafka accompany him back to Palestine. Leaves Prague with sister Elli and her children to stay at Mürtiz. Meets Tile Rössler, 16, and Dora Dymant, 19, the daughter of an Orthodox rabbi in Poland. Spends summer in Schelesen with sister Ottla. Becomes increasingly thin and ill. Moves with Dora to Berlin-Steglitz in September; at the end of the year they move to Grünewaldstrasse. Writes "A Little Woman" and "The Burrow." Attends lectures at the Academy for Jewish Studies. Becomes bedridden in December with fever.

1924   Moves with Dora to Heidestrasse in Berlin-Zehlendorf. Health declines rapidly. Klopstock and Max Brod bring Kafka back to Prague. Writes "Josephine, the Singer." Dora and Robert Klopstock travel with Kafka to Weiner Wald Sanatorium in

Ortmann, Austria. Illness intensifies. Barely able to speak. Publishes "Josephine" in the *Prager Presse* Easter issue. Moves to University Institute in Vienna, then to sanatorium at Kierling near Klosterneuburg. Receives letter from Dora's father denying permission to marry. On 2 June still working on "A Hunger Artist." Dies on 3 June. Buried in Jewish cemetery in Prague on 11 June. Memorial service held at Little Theater in Prague on 19 June.

LITERARY AND HISTORICAL CONTEXT

1

The History of an Image

With its anticipation of bureaucratic complexity, social isolation, and subjective emptiness in the twentieth century, *The Trial* can be regarded as an exemplary historical work of art. What is it we ask of a novel when we recognize its historical dimension and importance? We ask that, in the snapshot it furnishes of a time, a place, and a setting, it serve as an emblem and a summation of the world from which it arises; and we also ask that it exercise an *anticipatory* function, such that subsequent literary works granted "importance" by critical consensus "base" themselves upon it. The historical dimension of a novel is a peculiar combination of its monstrosity and its status as a model; of the initial singularity by which it dramatizes its era through striking imagery and stylistics; and of the authority it eventually asserts as a demonstrable paradigm for other works of art.

A historically significant novel thus *mirrors* history, *interprets* history, and *makes* history. In all of these senses, Franz Kafka's *The Trial* deserves the critical and historical importance it has been assigned. *The Trial* joins that brief list of artworks of which it may be said, in the words of the German critic Walter Benjamin, "all great works of literature found a genre or dissolve one . . . they are, in other words, special cases."[1]

The Trial plays a pivotal role in no less than three histories. In the history of world events and politics, its composition coincides with the pinnacle of the Austro-Hungarian Empire, the outbreak of World War I, and the subsequent dissolution of the empire and the decline of its political power and its sociopolitical and moral ideologies. Kafka's Prague vied with Budapest for the status of "second city" to Vienna during the Hapsburg dynasty. World War I, as it is implicated by Robert Musil's *The Man without Qualities,* was in part instigated over the question of which government and culture, Prussian or Austrian, would give the German-speaking world its impetus and direction.

In terms of the history of twentieth-century European literature, *The Trial* coincides with a far-reaching modernist experimentation concerned with the basic modes of language and the assumptions surrounding it that extended into virtually every genre and national literature. Kafka's particular questionings and explanations regarding such literary phenomena as plot, narrative posture and cohesion, characterization, fictive time, space, logic, and sentence structure can be mapped as part of the overall reconceptualization of fictive language carried out by, among others, James Joyce, Gertrude Stein, Marcel Proust, Virginia Woolf, William Faulkner, Robert Musil, and Ezra Pound. It would be safe to say that for Kafka's generation of literary experimenters, no literary assumptions or the philosophical concepts upon which they were based, were sacrosanct. Kafka's closest *compères* in literary history were encyclopedic not merely in the scale attained by certain of their monumental works (Proust's *In Remembrance of Things Past,* Musil's *The Man without Qualities,* Joyce's *Ulysses*), but in the persistence with which they challenged existing literary assumptions. Does the work express the intentions of its author? Must it be complete or even comprehensible? Are characters models of human thought, subjectivity, or psychology? Does the language of fiction have to say or communicate anything at all? What are the basic units of fictive works? In different ways, Kafka's generation of fictive explorers, who together with him comprise his particular moment of literary history, posited literary solutions to these and related questions. In its particular devices and improvisations, the body of Kafka's work may be regarded as a response to a set of questions shared by other writers of the moment whose novels and stories we remember and value.

There is yet a third important history to which *The Trial* belongs, and it offers the least coherence of all in terms of time and space. This is the history of the twentieth-century imagination, upon which Kafka's tone and mood, certain of the images around which he organized his fictive works, and his bearing to the literary image itself, exerted a profound and enduring influence. The history of the imagination or the imaginary is a difficult field in which to "establish" causalities or influences. It is not clear of what such "proofs" would consist. But the body of original and still disturbing literary works bearing the unique mark of Kafka's imagery and sensibility is a vast and important one. It encompasses, to name just a few of its most distinguished examples, Samuel Beckett's relentless fictive ruminations and the French *nouveau roman;* Bruno Schulz's uncanny reminiscences and Witold Gombrowicz's indirections of plot; the hopeless nostalgia occasionally escaping the critical observations of the Frankfurt school of criticism; the labyrinths of architecture, plot, and history explored by Jorge Luis Borges, Gabriel Garcia Márquez, and other writers of the "Latin American school"; the senses of space and death in the criticism of Maurice Blanchot and Georges Bataille; and the panorama opened by contemporary critical theory upon an endless space of textual configuration and disfiguration, articulation, and dissemination.

The Trial was begun, Ronald Hayman informs us, in July and August 1914.[2] The pivotal "Parable of the Doorkeeper," which serves as an allegorical "key" not only to the novel but to Kafka's wider understanding of the kinds of thinking and interpretation that take place in literature, was composed in December of that year. It is difficult to overemphasize the traumatic temperament of such a historical moment, especially when registered upon a sensibility as delicate as Kafka's. One of the great creative surges in his life, resulting in *The Trial,* coincided with the unexpected outbreak of World War I in July 1914. Its immediate pretext was the assassination of Archduke Franz Ferdinand, heir to the throne of Austria-Hungary, on 28 June, 1914, at Sarajevo, Bosnia. Wars, as the subsequent history of the twentieth century has taught us, are not the result of simple, single precipitating "causes." They do not incubate in a cloistered military domain. They arise in a setting of outmoded sociopolitical institutions, and as a result of stresses and strains in national, economic, and ethnic spheres. They become showcases for the latest technology that science has devised.

Kafka does not devote a lot of explicit attention to the Great War in his *Diaries* and other "more personal" writings. The war's complex motivations, however—such factors as nationalism, ethnic splitting, an economic downturn, class strife, burgeoning urban development—do enter and color the fictive worlds depicted in *The Trial* and Kafka's contemporaneous works. The examples are too numerous to be fully listed here, but I can mention the poverty of "The Bucket Rider" and the persecution evident in "Josephine the Singer, or the Mouse Folk."

Both the Great War and Kafka himself originated in a part of the world that put national and social institutions to a particular test. Central Europe, in Kafka's time and now again in our own (I think of recent events precipitated by the collapse of the Soviet Union and its former hegemony in the region) is home to populations large enough to lay claim to territory but not quite large enough to fulfill the demands made on modern nations. Kafka lived and wrote at a moment when serious doubts plagued the units and institutions of government in his region and throughout Europe. Is ethnic identity an adequate basis for nationality and social services? Is not capital the real basis for political divisions and processes? (Kafka's Uncle Alfred was an executive for the Spanish railways in Madrid.) To which institutions can an already splintered population turn to find equity and social justice?

World War I revealed the stress-lines produced by the competition between Germany and Austria-Hungary for domination of the German-speaking world. It released tensions between ethnic minorities ordinarily seething just beneath the surface. It accelerated the migration of Jews and other religious and ethnic groups from rural to urban areas, adding to the pressure on already overcrowded cities. (Kafka's

Diaries do chronicle the movements of Eastern Jews in and out of Prague.)

At the same time that the Great War underscored the bankruptcy of existing political units and social institutions, it stimulated and displayed the technology of the future: radio communication and the telephone; air, automobile, and modern train travel; the machine gun, gas, and other forms of indiscriminate mass killing. At the seminal moment of modernism in which Kafka lived and wrote, the means for unprecedented speed and accuracy in communications and transportation were becoming widely available. The Court in *The Trial* may be interpreted on one level as the legal-administrative embodiment and consummation of the particular technological level of development in Kafka's era. Will these advances be used for the purposes of sociopolitical enlightenment? Or will greedy officials and power-hungry splinter groups cynically deploy them to aggravate existing fragmentation and to increase the disparity between upper- and lower-class populations? These questions, and their obvious spinoffs, were very much "up for grabs" as Kafka went about writing *The Trial*. All three of Kafka's novels are very much pervaded by anxiety regarding their eventual answers. I can observe in advance of my interpretation of the novel (chapters 5–8)—from the Court's endless intrusiveness, the cynicism of its officials, and the cold-bloodedness of its henchman—that Kafka's outlook concerning the future was not overly optimistic.

For an overview of the interplay between politics, economics, and ideas in Kafka's part of the world at the turn of the century, I recommend Carl E. Schorske's *Fin-de-siècle Vienna: Politics and Culture*.[3] Schorske chronicles such factors as volatile political fragmentation, a gradual disenfranchisement of liberal parties and positions from the political process, major urban changes, including severe housing shortages, initiated by the construction of the Ringstrasse (a process extending, in different stages, from 1860 to almost 1900), and the political "trio" of radical anti-Semitic nationalism, Christian democracy, and Zionism, in accounting for the atmosphere prevailing in the empire during Kafka's formative years.

The rise of formidable bureaucratic organizations both in government and in private enterprise, a housing shortage not limited to

Vienna, electrification, and the dissemination of telephonic communication, the automobile, trains, and photography, are all developments that Kafka registers within the world of *The Trial,* for these developments were coincident with the period of its composition. Kafka records such technological changes both as an observer looking at his age (in 1909, on vacation in northern Italy, he had written the first account of an airplane published in German),[4] and because the increasing complexity of his moment embodied and expressed something very important to him about literature. It was well within Kafka's capability both to challenge and to question the organizational and technological developments permitting unprecedented assertions of authority and intrusions into "private" life—and simultaneously to marvel at the same phenomena as instances of the complexity that makes literature work and lies at the basis of its particular power. While the politics of the Austro-Hungarian Empire and the status and economic possibilities for Czechoslovakian Jews are surely historical "facts" underlying *The Trial* that must be reckoned with, technological developments such as the spread of telephones, photography, and electric-powered transportation may be even more important, because they mobilized in Kafka (and in Frankfurt school critics who were influenced by him, including Walter Benjamin and Theodor Adorno) one of the fundamental ambivalences of his age. This is a fascination with and recognition of the literary potential in the very same instruments of organization, communication, and transportation deployed under certain circumstances in the twentieth century for political repression, industrial dehumanization, urban chaos, and genocide.

In *Franz Kafka: Pictures of a Life,* the contemporary German critic Klaus Wagenbach has furnished us with an indispensable sourcebook.[5] Not only does this volume reproduce photographs of Kafka's immediate and extended families, and of the towns and villages where his ancestors originated and were buried, it also chronicles graphically such events and products as the transition from horse-drawn cars (1901) to electric (1905) trolley cars in Prague, the first phonographic exhibit held there (for the 1891 jubilee celebration), the one of 5,387 registered motorcycles in Czechoslovakia that Kafka borrowed from its owner, his uncle, Siegfried Löwy (1907), publicity from the above-mentioned airshow in Brescia, and the dismantlement and replacement, in 1893, of the old Prague Jewish ghetto.

The Court is a place where literary subtlety and the complexity of life in the twentieth century intertwine and become indistinguishable from each other. As Joseph K. learns from his lawyer, the Court painter Titorelli, and Block, his fellow defendant, the Court is as subtle and complicated as an intricate novel. Cutting oneself loose from its hold is tantamount to becoming a highly erudite and sensitive reader. The Court embodies many of the potentials for repression built into twentieth-century bureaucracy and technology; but its complexities and paradoxes—and, above all, the ability to interpret them—comprise the only possible means of liberation. Through the image of the Court, Kafka exemplifies the encompassing and bewildering potentials of twentieth-century organizations. But in the same image, he furnishes an unforgettable and breathtaking demonstration of the power and freedom inherent in finely wrought and fully explored literary images in well-crafted literature.

2

At the Crossroads of the Twentieth Century

Based on its broad receptivity to readers and the attitudes they bring to reading, *The Trial*'s importance may be articulated both internally and externally to Kafka's work. Within the body of Kafka's fiction, *The Trial* is surely his most sustained, intense, and cohesive novel, the latter, in spite of its "cloudy spots."[1] Kafka exploited the different characters and qualities made possible by the longer and shorter forms of fiction. He "played" these modes "off against" each other. His "short-short" fiction and some of his conventional-length stories are manifestly fragmentary. With significant exceptions (for example, "The Metamorphosis" and "A Hunger Artist"), Kafka offers us a menu consisting of whole fragments, or, in the case of the novels, of fragmentary wholes. One of his most coherent short stories in the conventional sense is "The Great Wall of China," whose subject matter, however, focuses on the breaks in the Great Wall, the impossible magnitude of its construction, and the absences in logic and communication that it occasions.

I have elsewhere argued that all of Kafka's major works consist in the elaboration of a single, encompassing image, whose effect upon the central character is both to confine him (or it) and to initiate him into the complexities of literary dynamics and language.[2] The particular power of *The Trial* to some extent derives from Kafka's choice of his (dis)organizing framework or metaphor. A court is an institution from "real life" endowed with a submerged stratum of professional knowledge. At the same time that Joseph K.'s Court will ultimately give evidence of an inhuman, monstrous, and fantastic dimension, the Court offices that K. penetrates are fictive variations on "real" ones; the lawyer and officials with whom he interacts are versions of "real" ones. In neither of Kafka's other two novels is the landscape for the protagonist's explorations and misadventures so specific or tangible. K. in *The Castle* tangles with the bureaucrats of an unspecified village government. The indefiniteness of the Castle's architecture spills over into the sequence of K.'s experiences and the structure of his interactions. *Amerika,* Kafka's earliest novel-length work, while sharing many of the political, psychosocial, and interpretative concerns common to all three novels, pursues a series of Karl Rossmann's interactions with authority, friendship, and sexual attraction and revulsion across an amorphous panorama of American vastness. While *Amerika* and *The Castle* may well be more whimsical and "fantastic" novels, *The Trial*'s relative "realism" and its fantasy both gain from their proximity to each other.

In terms of internal importance within the body of Kafka's writing, *The Trial* brings together into their most intense interplay three figures increasingly important both to Kafka's literary thought and to our own evolving understanding of its meaning. For the purposes of my present discussion, I shall call these figures, all elements of Kafka's creative self, the son, the martyr, and the artist. As his pained and lengthy *Letter to His Father*[3] attests, Kafka is very much the son of his family, his community, and his times. Although brutally healthy, assertive, arbitrary, and obtuse father-figures proliferate throughout Kafka's public and private writing, Hermann Kafka, who raised himself from a rural kosher butcher's son (his father's name was Joseph) to a wholesaler of dry goods in Prague, was less of a failure than might be evident from Franz Kafka's representations. The awesomeness of certain authority figures in Kafka's fiction arises less from the triviality of

Hermann Kafka's achievements than from his personal power and his success. Franz Kafka's own and third-person accounts leave little doubt that Hermann Kafka asserted his will and self-interest with bluntness and more than occasional cruelty. Temperamentally, the author's intellectual agility and personal delicacy, represented graphically in his line drawings, set him at loggerheads with his father. The interaction between Franz Kafka and his biographical father was a generational battle conditioned by different means of success, by opposed ways of coping, personal styles, gifts, and "weapons." Franz Kafka's self-representation in the battles of authority, profession, and self-fulfillment is often that of a frail, hypersensitive, misunderstood child. We could say that the figure of the martyr corresponds to Kafka's imaginary representation of himself as a perceptive son; and that art is an umbrella term for the field, devices, and defenses that the martyr mobilizes in his struggle for autonomy, self-assertion, integrity, and the redress of fundamental wounds. On an imaginary level, Kafka fragmented himself into an unholy trinity consisting of a son, a martyr, and an artist, an act all the more remarkable in light of his belonging to the precarious Jewish minority of an already minor German-speaking population in Prague, the latter consisting of only ten percent in the first decade of the century.

The workings of a triadic filial, messianic, and artistic sensibility are already evident in the precocious achievement of Kafka's youth, the 1905 novella, "Description of a Struggle."[4] Yet it was above all in 1912, the year of the two breakthrough works, "The Judgment" and "The Metamorphosis," that Kafka paved the way for the unique elaboration and interplay of these three figures in *The Trial*.

Given the shortness of Kafka's life and the relative size of his written corpus, his legacy to his followers is a remarkable one. Such a literary bequest is all the more striking given his repeated sense of writing as "a legacy from my father," a fate rather than an elective, something sharing the inevitability of birthmarks, mutations, and one's relatives. In one of Kafka's parables the narrator has fathered "Eleven Sons." Kafka's literary influences are to be numbered at far more than these. Several of them are evident in *The Trial*'s first sentence:

"Someone must have been telling lies about Joseph K., for without having done anything wrong he was arrested one fine morning" (*T*, 1). In its tone, this sentence already reveals much of the distinctly Kafkan ominousness, a sense that the worst has already and ineluctably transpired. Who is this "someone"? We can only *infer* that this hypothetical agent has been calumniating Joseph K., for the turn of events has taken place in an informational blackout. What Kafkan protagonists learn more often than not is the worst; and they do so in a setting indicated by this distinctive tone of vague, ubiquitous menace. Only hypotheses, the raw material of science fiction, can account for this downturn, this loss of empathic supports. For this reason, the *tonality* of many of Kafka's longer works links them to other ominous twentieth-century images of a forbidding future, in writers as diverse as George Orwell (*1984*), Aldous Huxley (*Brave New World*), and Jorge Luis Borges (*Ficciones*).

Like "The Metamorphosis," *The Trial* examines in a rational and comprehensive manner the implications of an irrational premise: that Joseph K., having committed no trespass of which he is aware, awakes one fine morning to find himself and his property wards of the Court. His first line of defense, like that of anyone confronted with a sudden and major change of basic life conditions, is to approach his new circumstances with his customary logic and common sense. *The Trial* devotes a significant portion of its narrative material to the successful resistance achieved by the Court and its procedures, traditions, legends, and officials to Joseph K.'s conventional logic and common sense. Like "The Metamorphosis," *The Trial* is a perfectly logical work about apprehensions and images ultimately refusing to submit to logic, whose nature is, above all, literary and aesthetic.

The first five chapters of the novel deal with Joseph K.'s incredulity, his outraged and somewhat contemptuous performance at a preliminary interrogation set in a Court installation housed in a tenement, his active efforts to master his circumstances by applying common sense to them and by penetrating the Court's customs and its very innards, and finally, the impact of the proceedings upon his personal and professional lives. His sexual interest seems to waken. The Court is so intrusive that in a storage closet in the bank where Joseph K.

works it punishes the warders who have invaded his home, eaten his breakfast, and appropriated his underwear.

The long central section of the novel, chapters 6–8, may be described as narrating Joseph K.'s draining education in the involuted and self-contradictory, but literarily paradigmatic, ways of the Court. In these chapters Joseph K. is instructed, among others, by Huld, the lawyer whom his Uncle Karl thrusts upon him, Titorelli, a Court painter, and Tradesman Block, a fellow defendant who has been reduced, after years of litigation, to a state of nervous exhaustion.

What Walter Benjamin terms a "cloudy spot,"[5] the ultimate affirmation of the novel's fragmentariness, separates these chapters from its doubled ending, chapter 9, in which a priest narrates to Joseph K. and then elucidates the Parable of the Doorkeeper, and chapter 10, in which two henchmen of the Court execute him. The Parable of the Doorkeeper affirms the ultimately literary quality of the Court that invades, preoccupies, and ultimately takes Joseph K.'s life. In this respect, it illuminates the paradoxical relationship between the artist's life and his work. To a certain extent, art, like Joseph K.'s trial, chooses its maker; builds itself into the recesses of his or her life; and exhausts that life while endowing it with its greatest intensity and vision. The Parable of the Doorkeeper thus serves as an ironic, and by no means definitive, caption on the enigmas unearthed by its protagonist throughout the novel—and on Kafka's distinctive understanding of the artistic process. It is succeeded by a description, made all the more horrifying by its matter-of-factness, of Joseph K.'s capital death. "Like a dog!" are his final words (T, 229). An intricate counterpoint between this sense of shame and a closely related contemptuous attitude furnishes a key to the novel's psychological dimension.

At the same time that *The Trial* playfully elaborates on logical possibilities, it is very much concerned with the nature and conditions of logic and its status within literary works. In this sense, *The Trial* spans both extremes of the seemingly contradictory investigation pursued by twentieth-century philosophy. On the one hand, it is very much of the style and world of that school of philosophy known as logical analysis. One of its major figures, the Viennese philosopher

Ludwig Wittgenstein (1889–1951) rigorously explored the borderline where logic and language both join and diverge from each other. This philosophy is a restrained but poetic attempt to say no more than can be justified logically, and to rigorously demarcate the domain where language, whether everyday or literary, necessarily deviates from logical specifications. Yet Joseph K. in *The Trial* also eventuates at a situation where the at-hand tools of reason and common sense are no longer sufficient to account for and control the paradoxical alogic shared by the Court and its parables. To the degree to which *The Trial* joins and dramatizes the insufficiency of logical superstructure, it also anticipates the movements of twentieth-century philosophy known as phenomenology, as exemplified by Martin Heidegger, and deconstruction, a variegated set of textual attitudes assembled by Jacques Derrida. In these latter approaches, philosophy sets aside its confinement to logical issues and statements and "acts out" the implications of its awareness of itself as an intellectual system constituted of language. Twentieth-century phenomenology and deconstruction are often considered antithetical in interest to analytical philosophy, and indeed, on superficial examination, they are. Phenomenological and deconstructive formulations are often couched in an expansive, elliptical style, punctuated by persistent qualifications, a method of expression that runs directly counter to the controlled, sequential order of logical deliberation.

Much of Kafka's fiction—and here *The Trial* plays a privileged role—unites the spare and the florid countertraditions of twentieth-century philosophy. *The Trial* is logically structured, and it pays careful attention to the logical status of its characters and their situations. In this respect, it may be described as philosophically analytical.

In the classical myth so central to modern psychology, Oedipus meets the man who is his father on the narrow footpath between the known and the unknown, between uncontrollable rage and inadmissable desire. As will become explicit in the reading of *The Trial* I offer, Kafka was very much the son of his family, his times, and his art. *The Trial* is situated at the crossroads of the twentieth century not merely because of its seemingly endless receptivity to intellectual approaches and interpretative models, but also because of its uncanny instinct for the literary experiments and devices from prior epochs that were to attain importance in its time, and because of the multifaceted—tonal, stylistic, environmental, logical, and narratological—influence it would assert upon a wide range of artworks in literature and other media.

3

The Trial of Interpretation and Its Critical Reception

Not only do "all great works of literature found a genre or dissolve one"; in a very powerful sense they structure the body of criticism that arises to receive, categorize, analyze, and assess them. Glossaries, bibliographies, and compendia of allusions and characters play an important role in the cohesion of a novel overflowing with neologisms, unmarked literary references, interlinguistic puns, and characters with multiple names such as Joyce's *Finnegans Wake*. *The Trial,* on the other hand, is written in a deceptively simple style and language. To the extent that its drama reaches any crowning climax or its text furnishes any key to its own meaning, this would be the Parable of the Doorkeeper, itself an allegory of interpretation, demonstrating how meanings and explanations supplant, contradict, and replace each other. What characterizes the critical literature arising in response to such a work is an extreme range and vitality of interpretative approaches. Within the dimensions of this chapter, I will be able to outline merely a few of the dominant interpretative models that have been or could be applied to *The Trial,* and I will furnish examples of these approaches. Of prime importance is the fact that the novel, in its own fascination with and dramatization of the interpretative process, established a particularly vibrant and inventive critical tradition from the time of its initial publication. The critical literature surrounding *The Trial* has incorporated virtually every fully elaborated intellectual movement or school of thought in subsequent twentieth-century intellectual history. Critical and artistic deliberation on *The Trial* continues. Its overall quality and its intensity and creativity show no signs of waning.

Who is on trial in *The Trial,* and for what offense? What is the nature of the trial? Is it a crisis of conscience? A ritual of alienation? A way station in the process of artistic creativity? Where is the trial set? In some uncanny mixture of office space and low-grade suburban Prague residential property? Does it take place, in other words, in some fictive *external* landscape? Or is its implicit setting *internal* or immanent, in the psyche or the soul, if such entities can be said to exist? Or is the fascination of the novel in part the multiple answers that these and similar questions sustain?

A point so basic that we might easily overlook it is the following: the answers to the above and related questions are very much contingent on the assumptions and intellectual models that the reader is bringing with him- or herself to the text. The identity of Joseph K., the nature of the Court and the trial, and the location and significance of other events change radically according to the reader's assumptions and methodological habits. If the reader focuses on the sociopolitical relationships depicted in the novel, the Court becomes a menacing power-machine; the trial is situated in the "external" world of society; and it objectifies some form of social alienation the reader can identify. These values change radically if the trial is assumed to be a psychological, or a theological, or a theoretical event. By the same token, each of these approaches will cite different passages from the novel in support of its hypotheses. Marxist and sociological readings may well stress chapters treating the officials and deliberations of the Court and the power and social relationships in the bank where Joseph K. works as chief clerk. Psychological approaches to *The Trial* will focus upon Joseph K.'s emotional states and his sexual infatuations; they regard power less as a function of some imaginary state or its corporate equivalent than as deriving from the structure of the nuclear family.

Structuralist and theoretical readings of the novel will find their point of entry in those chapters and passages that make explicit the novel's status as an artifact of patterned language whose intelligibility is made possible by signs, structures, and representation. The Parable of the Doorkeeper and Titorelli's paintings and his formulations of different types of acquittal hold an importance for theological, structuralist, and deconstructionist readings that they may not have for social and psychological approaches.

Just as the Parable of the Doorkeeper provides for an open-ended—virtually infinite—range of differing and at times mutually contradictory interpretations of itself, so too has *The Trial* sustained interpretations from every significant critical school or attitude of twentieth-century thought. In this surely consists its primary importance, its receptivity to commentary, its solicitation of the different frameworks and attitudes making up intellectual experience. Joseph K.'s circumstances and experiences are interesting from psychological, sociological, and political points of view. Kafka utilized his legal training on the staffs of worker's compensation insurance companies in Prague. As Klaus Wagenbach has stated, he was one of the few "bourgeois" writers of the century to incorporate the misery and suffering he encountered through his professional work into his fiction. A rich literature of Marxist interpretation has arisen in response to the novel. The irrationality and unpredictability of Court operations, the immediate pretext for the Parable of the Doorkeeper, bear striking similarities to Sigmund Freud's descriptions of the unconscious in *The Interpretation of Dreams*[1] (1900) and other works contemporaneous to Kafka's life and writing. *The Trial,* while belonging to the body of fantastic literature, is quite realistic from the perspective of twentieth-century psychological understanding. Its psychological verisimilitude surely constitutes a major element of its readerly appeal.

Kafka's choice of a legal setting for his novel endows it with a procedural or methodological dimension. *The Trial* is simultaneously both a paradigmatic work of fiction and a working example of the theories of literature and its criticism. It has sustained important interpretations from New Critical, structuralist, and deconstructionist points of view. A feminist exploration into the nature and implications of the sexual and power of relationships has begun.[2] *The Trial* is by the same token a fascinating artifact to all schools of philosophy and theology concerned with issues of exegesis and hermeneutics.

For purposes of the present introduction to the critical reception of *The Trial*, I should like to divide the scholarship into its general literary, psychoanalytical, sociopolitical, theological, theoretical, and biographical segments. Bearing in mind the needs of English-language readers, I will emphasize, without intending to slight others, contributions either written in English or available in translation. I have incorporated full bibliographical references into the text of this overview. I am indebted to Richard Jayne, a most creative scholar at Göttingen, whose death in 1991 constituted a serious loss to Kafka studies, for pointing me to some of the more recent additions to the critical literature.

One of the most distinctive features of Kafka's fictive writing is the proximity in which it places venerable literary traditions, philosophical argumentation, and a modernistic appreciation of language as the medium and structure for all artifacts and disciplines. The simultaneity with which Kafka deployed literary tradition, philosophy (even where he demolished logic), and linguistics was registered from the very outset by the critical and scholarly responses to his writing. The earliest and still one of the most brilliant contributions to the Kafka secondary literature, Walter Benjamin's essays and notes, at the same time registers Kafka's debt to the basic forms of myths and folktales and analyzes and dramatizes the radical distortion and updating Kafka performs upon them. Benjamin's major tribute to Kafka, commemorating the tenth anniversary of his death (in 1934), is itself a folktale or enigma of criticism at the same time that it surveys Kafka's foundations in myth, legend, parable, and Rabbinic *agadah*. Organized around the subversive figure of the literary image, which achieves both the elevated status of a self-enclosed ikon and the pandemonium of shock, Benjamin's essay, "Franz Kafka: On the Tenth Anniversary of His Death," nevertheless relates Kafka's experimentation to the overall sociohistorical progression in which experience declines and dreams and art lose their aura in a world of mechanical reproduction and modernistic chaos. Benjamin's approach to Kafka is prophetic of later general literary commentaries. Deriving its inspiration from Kafka's works themselves, Benjamin's reading applies literary categories (in this case generic ones), philosophical concepts (for example, history), and extraliterary frameworks (in this case society) at the same time to the fictive works (Benjamin, 111–46). Literature alone has rarely been considered an adequate scholarly instrument in the history of Kafka criticism. Literary approaches to Kafka have preeminently submitted to the impulse to yoke or place in tandem some literary point of view (genre or rhetoric) with philosophical concepts (for example, reality or truth) and/or with extraliterary frameworks (for example, society, the psyche, or religion). Kafka criticism has attained a certain distinction on the basis of its attempt to gain mastery over Kafka's enigmatic writings through the establishment of a parallelism between interpretative perspectives, each insufficient in its own right but in combination creating a sense of comprehensiveness. This inclusiveness has become an earmark of Kafka criticism, even coloring the present introduction to *The Trial* in which I associate the filial, the artistic, and the messianic in Kafka's writing. The titles of the overarching academic studies that began to appear in the 1960s bear this point out.

The high overall quality of Kafka studies from the outset has been in large part due to this fundamental dissatisfaction with any single approach, tradition, or set of intellectual tools. Since Kafka began to attract sustained intellectual interest, with the republication and translation of his novels in the late 1930s, he has been a comparatist's writer par excellence, if by comparative literature we mean the quest for meaning and significance *between* the spheres delineated by national literatures and academic disciplines. The titles of two earlier big studies that I can recommend, Heinz Politzer's *Franz Kafka: Parable and Paradox*[3] and Walter Sokel's *Franz Kafka: Tragik und Ironie*[4] hover between categories of literary form (parable and tragedy) and rhetoric (paradox and irony). They indicate how from the beginning Kafka scholarship has found it necessary to approach the metacritical problem of language while taking up considerations of form, allusion, and concept. A third important groundbreaking treatment from this era, Wilhelm Emrich's *Franz Kafka: A Critical Study of His Writings*,[5] evenly divides the intellectual context for discussing Kafka between philosophy ("The Universal Thema," "Man's 'Self' ") and rhetoric (symbol and allegory). General literary studies of Kafka have never abandoned this comparative or mixed approach. It is no doubt solicited by the interpretative multiplicity dramatized by the Parable of the Doorkeeper and its various readings.

Kafka's fiction, because of its solid grounding in the history of world literature, has from the beginning of its dissemination appealed to professed literary critics, to that near-extinct breed of writers, including Edmund Wilson and Maurice Blanchot, whose avowed vocation consisted in representing the interests of an informed readership in the midst of fluctuating literary innovation. Wilson's reception, "A Dissenting Opinion of Kafka," reprinted in the Twentieth Century Views collection *Kafka: A Collection of Critical Essays,*[6] is frankly skeptical. Blanchot devoted considerable attention to Kafka, above all in his 1955 *The Space of Literature.*[7] For Blanchot, as for the French authors of the *nouveau roman* and *cinéma,* Kafka furnishes a setting in which it becomes possible to endow the senses of despair, morbidity, and meaninglessness prompted by the major events of twentieth-century history with some genuine philosophical rigor. According to Blanchot, Kafka synthesizes a literary medium, configures a literary space, and elaborates an attitude toward death that constitutes a major literary response to modern brutality and despair. Blanchot's notions of writing, death, and space straddle the border between philosophy and literature. These concerns will resurface in the considerable number of theoretical approaches to which Kafka's fiction later gave rise.

The writings of Theodor Adorno on Kafka, by the same token, occasion many subsequent socially oriented interpretations of his work. Adorno joins Walter Benjamin in placing Kafka's work in the most rigorous philosophical, historical, and sociopolitical contexts possible. This shuttling back and forth between different interpretative indices is the hallmark of Frankfurt school and successful contemporary cultural studies approaches. Adorno, in his "Notes on Kafka,"[8] wrestles with the paradox that the various forms of deviance that Kafka dramatizes in *The Trial* and other works may in fact be normative for his historical and intellectual age.

As literary scholarship strove for higher degrees of definition in the 1970s and 1980s, and began to approach more specialized audiences, general literary approaches to Kafka continued to perform a balancing act incorporating literary history and form and philosophical and linguistic concepts. An outstanding later example in this vein, one particularly useful with regard to the theatrical metaphor I discuss in chapter 5, is James Rolleston's *Kafka's Narrative Theater.* "For Kafka," Rolleston writes, "the theatrical metaphor is implicit in the very act of writing."[9] In a general literary vein surely the following volumes will also be indispensable in preparing the reader, shedding particular refractions of light upon Kafka's work: Ronald Gray's *Franz Kafka,*[10] Anthony Thorlby's *Kafka: A Study,*[11] Günther Anders's *Franz Kafka,*[12] and Walter Sokel's *Franz Kafka.*[13]

From a psychoanalytical point of view, *The Trial* and other of Kafka's writings are rich enough to have encompassed both of the major theoretical models according to which modern psychology has aligned itself, namely, Freud's classical "drive/structure" model and the theories of object-relations and personality disorders. *The Trial* may be interpreted convincingly both in the Freudian sense of Joseph K.'s oedipal conflict with figures and institutions of authority (for example, the examining magistrate, the Doorkeeper), his fluctuating sexuality, and his increasing morbidity. Yet as I will demonstrate in chapters 7–9, the novel also prefigures the psychoanalytic theory in which the presence or absence of empathy in the psychosexual environment predicates behavior more significantly than drives, developmental stages, or sexual symbology.

A solid conventional Freudian reading of *The Trial* is to be found in Walter Sokel's "The Programme of K.'s Court: Oedipal and Existential Meanings of *The Trial.*"[14] One of the great psychoanalytical French critics has also written extensively on Kafka. In *Franz Kafka's Loneliness,*[15] Marthe Robert's approach to our author is psychoanalytical in the broadest sense of the term. She devotes as much attention to Kafka's tortured relationships to his own Jewish, familial, marital, and social identities as she does to his conflict with his brutal, domineering father. Her result is an engagement with Kafka and his work still recognizable primarily in terms of psychoanalysis's dominant tradition. A useful transitional study, firm in its Freudian principles but pointing the way to subsequent psychological models, is Calvin S. Hall and Richard E. Lind's *Dreams, Life, and Literature: A Study of Franz Kafka.*[16]

The vicissitudes of Joseph K. in *The Trial,* Georg Bendemann in "The Judgment," and Gregor Samsa in "The Metamorphosis" are at the same time discernible and interpretable in terms of later psychologists of the self, whose work drew its inspiration from, among other sources, the interpersonal approach of Harry Stack Sullivan, the ego psychology of Heinz Hartmann, and the object-relations work of Melanie Klein, W. R. D. Fairbairn, D. W. Winnicott, and Margaret Mahler. For Heinz Kohut, whose work, along with that of Otto Kernberg, has been of inestimable service to me in reassessing *The Trial* in the current volume, "it is the understimulated child, the insufficiently responded-to child, the daughter deprived of an idealizable mother, the son deprived of an idealizable father, that has now become paradigmatic for man's central problem in our Western world, so it is the crumbling, fragmenting, enfeebled self of this child and later, the fragile, vulnerable, empty self of the adult that the great artists of the day describe—through time and word, on canvas and in stone—and that they try to heal."[17] Kafka becomes for Kohut the consummate modern poet of a devalued, fragmented, morose self. In the same passage from *The Restoration of the Self* cited immediately above, he writes:

> Gregor Samsa, the cockroach in Kafka's *The Metamorphosis,* may serve here as an example. He is the child whose presence in the world had not been blessed by the empathic welcome of selfobjects—he is the child of whom his parents speak impersonally, in the third-person singular; and now he is a nonhuman monstrosity, even in his own eyes. And Kafka's K., the Everyman of our time, engages in an endless search for meaning. He tries to get close to the great ones in power (the adults, the parents who reside in *The Castle*), but he cannot reach them. And in *The Trial* he perishes, still searching for a redeemable, at least for an understandable guilt—the guilt of Man yesterday. He cannot find it; and thus he dies a meaningless death—"like a dog." (287–88)

Such is Joseph K.'s predicament within the purview of his interpersonal landscape, as he interacts with his primary objects; no longer as he functions within a schema of preexisting structures and preplotted instincts and drives.

Social approaches to Kafka and *The Trial* are all, directly or not, descended from the concerns raised by Benjamin and the Frankfurt school. This is true of social treatments retaining a psychoanalytical element, above all Gilles Deleuze and Félix Guattari's excellent *Kafka: Toward a Minor Literature.*[18] This volume surveys the psychological as well as the philosophical and sociological dimensions of marginal writing, a pseudogenre that Kafka, in the authors' terms, founded and exemplified. Early socially oriented studies, such as Mark Spilka's *Dickens and Kafka: A Mutual Interpretation,*[19] are struck by Kafka's attention to poverty and misery, to the confinement of the Kafkan hero within imprisoning spaces and environments. Franz Kuna, in *Kafka: Literature as Corrective Punishment,*[20] associates key elements in Kafka's subject matter and fictive technique with notions, long-standing as well as contemporary, of writing as an expiation for sin and bad faith. Kuna locates Kafka's attitudinal models in the German philosopher Max Stirner (1806–56), Leo Tolstoy, Leopold Sacher-Masoch, and Hofmannsthal's *The Letter of Lord Chandos.* Kuna treats the name of Gregor Samsa, hero of "The Metamorphosis," as a construct fusing the appellation "Kafka" with "Sacher-Masoch." His study situates itself in a space immediately accessible to the archaeological view of history that Michel Foucault will expound, among other places, in *Discipline and Punish.*[21] Recent work in cultural studies applies multiple theoretical perspectives, all with social implications, to literary works. I heartily recommend Jack Murray's *The Landscape of Alienation: Ideological Deconstruction in Kafka, Céline, and Onetti.*[22] Murray teases out the political and ideological implications of the bleak landscape so prominent throughout Kafka's novels.

The remoteness of the sources and holders of power and the inscrutability of the Law have made Kafka's novels, ever since their first appearance, particularly susceptible to theological interpretation. Until recently, theological or closely related existential approaches have focused on the absence of divinity, purity, and meaning in the universe of Kafka's fiction. Later studies, as we shall see, draw upon deeply entrenched traditions of theological disputation for a model of the interpretation and hermeneutics that such works as *The Trial* and *The Castle* set into play. An early exploration in this direction, known at least in part to Benjamin, is Robert Rochefort's *Kafka où l'Irréductible espoir.*[23] Paul Goodman, in *Kafka's Prayer,*[24] emphasizes the meditative qualities of Kafka's aphorisms and the issues of freedom, self-destruction, and constructiveness raised by his fiction. Charles Neider's work of the same period, *The Frozen Sea,*[25] explores Kafka's writing in terms of the cabala and mystical and sexual unions. Martin Greenberg's *The Terror of Art: Kafka and Modern Literature*[26] reads *The Trial* as a religious allegory of personal responsibility. Joseph K. stands before an "unjust" divine tribunal. Gregor Samsa in "The Metamorphosis" suffers the inherent limitations in modern spiritual life. Michel Carrouges's *Kafka versus Kafka,*[27] is yet another of the major contributions to the tradition of theologically inspired existential despair.

Such a contemporary reading as Jill Robbins's "Kafka's Parables" in her *Prodigal Son/Elder Brother*[28] skirts the conventional theological Sturm und Drang in favor of a well-informed extrapolation of the hermeneutic positions implicit in Kafka's fiction. Theology's tradition leaves an indelible mark on Kafka, argues Robbins, not in the spectacle of his characters' doubts and suffering but in the form of the exquisite interpretative play and riddles that his parables dramatize. Robbins's gift for fleshing out the positions implicit in interpretative fables has helped me to discern with greater clarity the interplay between the Kafkan son, artist, and martyr.

So "aware" is Kafka's fiction of its linguistic qualities and status, so successful is the simultaneity that Kafka achieves between storytelling and textual allegory, that it is no wonder that the dissemination of critical theory and a more philosophically informed bearing to literature in the late 1960s and 1970s brought about a major resurgence of interest in Kafka's work. In many senses, Kafka is the deconstructionist's writer par excellence. The Parable of the Doorkeeper in *The Trial,* the Castle bureaucracy, the execution machine in "In the Penal Colony," and "The Great Wall of China"—all activate the conditions and production of writing in a remarkably rigorous way. A harbinger in this direction was Stanley Corngold's *The Commentator's Despair: The Interpretation of Kafka's "Metamorphosis."*[29] The author of the present volume owns the dubious distinction of having written one of the first fully deconstructive treatments of the *The Trial,* at least in the English language, "The Court as Text: Inversion, Supplanting, and Derangement in Kafka's *Der Prozeß.*[30] Certain issues such as the Court's inclusiveness, its combination of a stifling atmosphere and wild interpretative variance, and its devastating impact upon its central character's everyday life will be taken up in chapters 5–8. In *Franz Kafka: Geometrician of Metaphor,*[31] which includes the essay on *The Trial,* I expanded the discussion to incorporate Kafka's overall approach to fictive language in the short works as well as the novels. Kafka emerges from this study as a formidable theoretician, whose explorations and inventions anticipated many of the techniques that his fellow modernists devised and much of the conceptual work underlying the Frankfurt school, French structuralism as exemplified by Barthes, Foucault, and Lévi-Strauss, and poststructuralism and the theory of deconstruction.

Theoretical reconsiderations of Kafka have tended to identify language and the linguistic field as the ultimate courtroom or arena in which the conflicts that Kafka's works set into play are decided. This is a departure from the initial major treatments, such as those by Politzer, Sokel, and Emrich, which, although attentive to linguistic issues, tended to subordinate them to psychological, sociological, formal, and biographical considerations. It is perhaps no exaggeration to claim that critical theory, despite its questioning of causality, has determined the course of Kafka criticism over the past 15 years. A collection suggesting the full range of possible theoretical interventions, edited by Alan Udoff, is *Kafka and the Contemporary Critical Performance,*[32] with major essays by Jacques Derrida, Rainer Nägele, Avital Ronell, and Alan Udoff. In *Flaubert and Kafka,*[33] Charles Bernheimer surveys the interstices between textual and psychological structure. The major current German study of Kafka from a theoretical point of view may well be Hans Helmut Hiebel's *Die Zeichen des Gesetzes: Recht und Macht bei Franz Kafka.*[34] In recent theoretical work, Stanley Corngold consolidates and enlarges upon earlier offerings in *Kafka: The Necessity of Form*[35]; Clayton Koelb looks at the author from a comprehensive rhetorical point of view in *Kafka's Rhetoric: The Passion of Reading*[36]; and I place Kafka in the wider contexts of modernist *bricolage* and postmodern indifference, exploring Kafka's interactions with Wittgenstein, Joyce, Beckett, and Borges, among others, in *Afterimages of Modernity: Structure and Indifference in Twentieth-Century Literature.*[37] An ingenious French contribution to the theoretical literature has been Jean-Michel Rey's *Quelqu'un danse: Les Noms de F. Kafka.*[38]

With regard to biographical resources, in my opinion the richest by far consists of the photographs, letters, and documents that Klaus Wagenbach has assembled in his *Franz Kafka: Pictures of a Life.* A fine source for *The Trial* in terms of manuscript reproduction is Malcolm Pasley and Ulrich Ott's *Franz Kafka, Der Prozeß: Die Handschrift redet.*[39] The three "classical" biographical portraits of Kafka are by his friend, Max Brod, *Franz Kafka: A Biography*[40]; the son of a colleague at the Workmen's Accident Insurance Institution, who interviewed him, Gustav Janouch, *Conversations with Kafka*[41]; and by his best archivist, Klaus Wagenbach, *Franz Kafka: Eine Biographie seiner Jugend.*[42] Nobel Prize–winner Elias Canetti, whose career spanned Kafka's generation and our own, dedicated a volume to Kafka's agonizing relationship with his ur-fiancée, *Kafka's Other Trial: The Letters to Felice.*[43] A biography whose method largely consists of charting Kafka's life on the basis of his autobiographical notations in the *Diaries* and correspondence is Ronald Hayman's *Kafka: A Biography.* The latest contribution to the biographical literature, one coordinated with readings of the major works, is Pietro Citati's *Kafka.*[44]

The multiplicity of interpretations that Kafka's writing solicits has long embodied itself in the form of excellent essay collections focusing on various aspects of his work. In addition to *Kafka and the Contemporary Critical Performance*, cited above, I recommend as background to *The Trial* and in alphabetical order the following: Harold Bloom, ed., *Franz Kafka's "The Trial"*[45]; Angel Flores, ed., *The Kafka Problem*[46]; Ronald Gray, ed., *Kafka*[47]; Kenneth Hughes, ed., *Franz Kafka: An Anthology of Marxist Criticism*, an excellent introduction to sociopolitical approaches to Kafka[48]; Franz Kuna, ed., *On Kafka: Semi-Centenary Approaches*[49]; James Rolleston, ed., *Twentieth-Century Interpretations of "The Trial"*[50]; and J. P. Stern, ed., *The World of Franz Kafka.*[51] As this volume goes to press yet another important anthology has appeared, Ruth V. Gross's *Critical Essays on Franz Kafka,*[52] with the pivotal "policy statements" of several of the major current Kafka critics.

There is no indication whatsoever that Kafka is being relegated to the sideshow of critical and literary exploration. On the contrary, as criticism enlarges and revises the repertory of its concerns, Kafka's work proves indomitable in eliciting innovative, experimental responses.

A READING

4

Rehearsals

Literary interpretation, even where it questions its methods and working assumptions, strives to achieve a narrative coherence not entirely unlike the novelist's. The reading of *The Trial* in this volume draws much of its cohesiveness from the interplay between aspects of Kafka's living, working, and imaginary self, his status as son, martyr, and artist. The purpose of the framework is not merely classificatory, like the system of mail distribution in *The Castle*. Such a division and coordination of facets of the self (with an emphasis on Kafka's artistic emanation) allows for radical discrepancies in fictive moods, settings, and incidents to be seen against the background of some broader integration and artistic transformation of personal experience. The shameful pain of Joseph K.'s death at the end of *The Trial*, for example, draws both upon common childhood experiences of being the least powerful and most insignificant member in an at times hostile family environment and upon the veneration and sympathy for martyrs evident in a broad range of world cultures and religions. It is as a son that Joseph K. dies, but he is prepared for this most devastating of experiences by an extension of his *artistic* sensibility, the gloss on the Parable of the Doorkeeper, furnished not unsignificantly by a *priest*. We may say in the end that art, and a literary sensitivity to the proliferation and supplanting of meanings at the heart of texts, prepares Joseph K. for an eventuality that his status as a son, a striving-desiring subject like anyone else, simply cannot assimilate.

From within this overall framework, we will be looking carefully at the tenor and details of Joseph K.'s fictive experience. Before proceeding to the novel, however, I will devote the present chapter to discussing Kafka's preparations for this existential-artistic division of labor in the short fiction now assembled between the covers of *The Complete Stories*. I do this not as a scholarly or academic exercise, but because Kafka himself, in the experimental, self-revising nature of his fiction, formulated the most illuminating "key" to his novels. The parables and short stories of *The Complete Stories* may be read as glosses on the novels and vice versa. In this sense, Kafka was his own best critic and theorist, something that, as someone who has written extensively about his work in a theoretical vein, I freely admit. In this chapter, then, we will be reviewing, briefly and incompletely, certain of the rehearsals for the unholy Kafkan trinity consisting of son, martyr, and artist found in *The Complete Stories*. Certain of the parables and stories we will be considering appeared during the author's lifetime, largely in literary journals and anthologies edited in Prague, Vienna, Munich, Leipzig, and Berlin. Others were reserved until Kafka's friend and literary executor, Max Brod, together with Hans-Joachim Schoeps, edited a posthumous collection whose title translates as *The Great Wall of China: Unpublished Stories and Prose from the Literary Remains,* which appeared in Berlin in 1931.[1]

The most interesting fragmentary works to read in conjunction with *The Trial* concern the nature and transmission of guilt; the legacy of art and the artistic sensibility; art as a negation of or resistance to the appetites and exigencies of everyday life; the generational battle between father and son and the perspectival dissonance it engenders; and a complex cat-and-mouse game parallel, but not identical, to it— between the artist and his practical-minded handlers and managers. In these works—among them "The Knock at the Manor Gate," "The Cares of a Family Man," "The Judgment," "The Metamorphosis," "First Sorrow," and "A Hunger Artist"—emerges a configuration in which the son's importance and not entirely welcome responsibility parallels the artist's giftedness, sensitivity, and self-sacrifice, which in turn result in a martyrdom of suffering and possible death.

"And one of the superstitions is that you're supposed to tell from a man's face, especially the line of his lips, how his case is going to turn out. Well, people declared that judging from the expression of your lips you would be found guilty, and in the near future too," recounts the shell-shocked Tradesman Block to Joseph K. in chapter 8 of *The Trial* (*T*, 174). According to this account, Joseph K.'s guilt is a matter of expression more than deed; it is a foregone conclusion long before the trial reaches any definitive result. Guilt, for Kafka, is an uneluctable family legacy. In this respect, it parallels the aesthetic calling. In "The Knock at the Manor Gate," one of Kafka's posthumously published fables, a brother and a son assumes the guilt for a misdeed of his sister so trivial that it may not have taken place at all, to discover by the end of this intense two-page piece that he has been condemned to die in a medieval setting of torture. As a psychological phenomenon, guilt is, for Kafka, hopelessly foregone. It is retrospective in stance and transferable from one family member to another (a displacement that also transpires within Barnabas's family in *The Castle*). Only according to the predatory logic of guilt could a completely trivial offense, quite literally a nothing, be transferred from sister to brother and result in an irreversible death sentence. What is unbelievable from a standpoint of common sense makes a superb, condensed short-short story. Kafka has in effect taught us that in the domain of the literary image, the Newtonian symmetry between cause and effect no longer applies.

"I cannot tell now whether she knocked on the gate out of mischief or out of absence of mind, or merely threatened it with her fist and did not knock at all" (*CS*, 418). With these words, the brother and son describes the human failing of a sibling who has already determined his downfall. "A hundred paces further on along the road" (*CS*, 418) this pair, whose innocence is assured by the taboos of incest (what is more pure and boring than "kissing your sister"?) enters a purgatorial scene painted in forbidding and romantic colors, a world of menacing gestures and abrupt, unmotivated acts, a world fitted out with traits from all three of Kafka's novels on a miniature scale.

No sooner had we passed the first house when people appeared and made friendly or warning signs to us; they were themselves apparently terrified, bowed down with terror. They pointed toward the manor house that we had passed and reminded us of the knock on the gate. The proprietor of the manor would charge us with it, the interrogation would begin immediately. I remained quite calm and also tried to calm my sister's fears. Probably she had not struck the door at all, and if she had, nowhere in the world would that be a reason for prosecution. I tried to make this clear to the people around us; they listened to me but refrained from passing any opinion. Later they told me that not only my sister, but I too, as her brother, would be charged. I nodded and smiled. We all gazed back at the manor, as one watches a distant smoke cloud and waits for the flames to appear. And right enough we presently saw horsemen riding in through the wide-open gate. Dust rose, concealing everything. (CS, 418)

Particularly ominous in this passage are the villagers' "friendly or warning signs," suggesting not much difference between these possible messages, and their terror; the speed at which the events unfold; and the proprietor's readiness for an interrogation. The narrator's impulse, to remain "quite calm" and banish the chimeras of emotion, is quite characteristic of the protagonists in Kafka's novels, that is, until they themselves are overcome, whether by the irrationality of the events and conditions around them or by the unsuspected bad faith they discover in themselves. Under the duress of spear-carrying horsemen, the innocence of the siblings and their concern for each other's safety is both touching and hopeless. "I urged my sister to leave me, I myself would set everything right. She refused to leave me. I told her that she should at least change, so as to appear in better clothes before these gentlemen. At last she obeyed and set out on the long road to our home. Already the horsemen were beside us" (CS, 418). It is up to the son of the family to set everything right. The son finally achieves his mission, to extract his sister from the menacing scene, by involving the social codes of modesty and proper appearance. This act of heroism isolates him and exposes him in a vulnerable state to an authoritarian law whose dictates are carried out with a mixture of cruelty ("The room looked more like a prison cell than the parlor of a farmhouse"

[*CS*, 419]), insensitivity ("The answer was received almost with indifference" [*CS*, 418]), and unyielding rigidity ("the judge . . . already awaiting me, said: 'I'm really sorry for this man'" [*CS*, 419]).

Visually, "The Knock at the Manor Gate" translates into a purgatorial canvas on a miniature scale by one of the early Flemish masters (I think of Bosch or Cranach). For the purposes of our reading of *The Trial*, I am most interested in the situation of the brother and son, and how he is transformed, simply by exercising his good sense and enforcing well-established social codes of modesty and male responsibility, into a martyr. As this fable suggests, there is not an overwhelming distance separating filial duty (can we speak of sonliness?) from a maimed exercise of self-interest, and ultimately personal disaster, experienced as self-sacrifice. The good son is quickly transformed into a martyr, the story suggests. (This does not take place entirely at the expense of the sister's good faith. "She refused to leave me," but then, acquiescing to some law binding both siblings, she does depart from the scene, leaving the son exposed. Could the male narrator resent her assumed immunity?) Guilt is the issue motivating the brother's confrontation with the Law. The minitrial that the narrator undergoes takes place in order to establish his guilt. In the scenario emerging from "The Knock at the Manor Gate," guilt emanating from the sister and possibly from other quarters of the family radiates toward the son, who becomes, in effect, the family guilt-collecter. I should mention, in this regard, that Kafka was the only surviving male among four siblings, of which he was the oldest by a good margin. Franz's brother Georg died in 1885, while still a baby. Sisters Elli, Valli, and Ottla (his favorite and confidante) were, respectively, six, seven, and nine years younger. Franz Kafka was the only male counterpart and counter in the brood to his father's industry, energy, egotism, and considerable personal power.

"The Knock at the Manor Gate" does not specify much about the authority that the children have evidently enraged. It is, evidently, arbitrary, speedy, and coldly punitive. In other works, notably the novels, Kafka elaborates the sensibility and logic (or their absence) with which the Law enforces its dictates and instructs its servants. This short-short story is, however, most suggestive of why in Kafka's fiction the figure of the son is but a stone's throw away from that of the martyr; why the son is almost already, with the implacable logic of our fable, martyred.

Guilt and punishment are not, however, the son's only legacies. The figure of the son also inherits his artistic calling or predisposition. In two of Kafka's fables "A Crossbreed [A Sport]" and "The Cares of a Family Man" (the latter published twice during the author's lifetime), the narrator inherits a legacy whose self-negating logic and composition out of diverse and indifferent (if not opposed) elements qualifies it as a work (or activity) of art. In both tales, the narrator is put to some inconvenience simply in deciphering his inheritance. Both tales specify that the narrator's relationship to his patrimony, whether the kitten/lamb of "A Crossbreed" or the hybrid speaking composition, fashioned of animate and inanimate parts in "The Cares of a Family Man," is a decidedly pained and belabored one. Both texts associate art with striking and anomalous combination, and a certain morbid temperament with the aesthetic sensibility. Brief as these fragments are, then, each taking up hardly a good page, they both mobilize the elements of the son-artist-martyr triad.

A legacy is a fate, an imposition. It is a demand extracted from the future, and yet it is experienced as an afterthought. The narrators of "A Crossbreed" and "The Cares of a Family Man" approach their respective patrimonies with a brooding air of finality, similar in its absoluteness to Joseph K.'s arrest and Gregor Samsa's transformation into an insect *before* the narration of the texts in which they are registered has begun. Resignation is the mode in which the Kafkan protagonist experiences inheritance and tradition as obligation or guilt; and in which he accepts artistic giftedness as a calling. Family tradition and artistic talent evoke the full range of ambivalence triggered by the gift.[2]

As both stories progress, the narrator's rapport with his inheritance or his gift evolves from otherness and estrangement to a certain mirroring or complicity. These fables begin in a sense of the detached puzzlement aroused by any well-conceived riddle and end in a solemn conspiracy between partners in the artwork, between the writer and his language. This partnership combines the intimacy of near-total familiarity with the resolve of a suicide pact, a marriage unto death.

In "A Crossbreed" the son's inheritance consists of a kitten/lamb hybrid that delights in defying the logical as well as the biological categories to which it belongs.

> I have a curious animal, half kitten, half lamb. It is a legacy from my father. But it only developed in my time; formerly it was far more lamb than kitten. Now it is both in about equal parts. From the cat it takes it head and claws, from the lamb its size and shape; from both its eyes, which are wild and flickering, its hair, which is soft, lying close to its body, its movements, which partake both of skipping and slinking. Lying on the window sill in the sun it curls up in a ball and purrs; out in the meadow it rushes about like mad and is scarcely to be caught. It flees from cats and makes to attack lambs. On moonlight nights its favorite promenade is along the eaves. It cannot mew and it loathes rats. Beside the hen coop it can lie for hours in ambush, but it has never yet seized an opportunity for murder. (*CS,* 426)

So fascinating are the possibilities for logical play offered by this complex puzzle endowed with literary form that we overlook the specifications, "it is a legacy from my father. But it only developed in my time" (*CS,* 426). The kitten/lamb is a veritable knot of contradictions. At the beginning of the text, these focus around the incompatibility between its carnivorous and ruminative qualities, but by the end, the creature defies logical categories in general. In the opening paragraph, Kafka describes the creature at once as *both* a kitten and a lamb, *either,* and *neither.* He tries to disqualify all readily at hand logical (and grammatical) possibilities for pidgeonholing the thing. The creature is there: it is one of the narrator's possessions or attributes. Yet it cannot resolve its internal contradictions. This is what endows it with a hopelessly creepy quality. "In long droughts it sucks the milk in through its fang-like teeth."

This story vacillates between the playfulness afforded by the creature's originality and the morbidity of its solitude and the narrator's pact with it. "Sometimes I cannot help laughing when it sniffs around me and winds itself between my legs and simply will not be parted from me. Not content with being a lamb and cat, it almost insists on being a dog as well" (CS, 427). The aesthetic joy occasioned by the creature consists in the creative possibilities that it opens up, which are so numerous as to defy categorization. The creature disqualifies even the apparent categories (the species of cats and sheep) by which it makes itself intelligible. But this creative joy comes at the expense of guilt, the sense of having violated some pre-existing law.

> Its skin feels too tight for it. Sometimes it jumps up on the arm-chair beside me, plants its front legs on my shoulder, and puts its muzzle to my ear. It is as if it were saying something to me, and as a matter of fact it turns its head afterwards and gazes in my face to see the impression its communication has made. And to oblige it I behave as if I had understood, and nod. Then it jumps to the floor and dances about with joy.
>
> Perhaps the knife of the butcher would be a release for this animal; but as it is a legacy I must deny it that. So it must wait until the breath voluntarily leaves its body, even though it sometimes gazes at me with a look of human understanding, challenging me to do the thing of which both of us are thinking. (CS, 427)

The sin of the son's foregone legacy, which it shares through implicit understanding with the son, is a skin "too tight for it." Of crucial importance to the above passage is the near-silent but implicit communication between the son and his artistic legacy. We may think of the creature as the narrator's "mark of art" (as opposed to "mark of Cain"). It "belongs" to the narrator, yet has an existence and an expression independent from him. According to the fable's involuted, near-perverse logic, the creature must suffer the *punishment* of endurance, of life, because it is an extension of the narrator. The *simplicity* for which it yearns, and which would enter it in the form of a butcher's knife, is withheld from it. The narrator is fated, through his legacy, to suffer his own internal incompatibility with himself and his compatriots; the *creature* of his singularity and artistic calling, on the other hand, is fated to suffer the endurance of these conditions, until the condition of death, morbidly desired, reestablishes simplicity. The life of art, which is both the son's weapon (or defense) and an imposition, consists of a fluctuation between the moods of joyous discovery and morbid fatalism.

The connection between such a spare and stark fable and *The Trial,* Kafka's most realistic and fully elaborated novel, may not be obvious, but it is very powerful nonetheless. Joseph K. does not, at least apparently, wish for his trial, yet it is his anyway. Mounting a legal defense, like owning the crossbreed, is an exercise in paradox, contradiction, and the proliferation of interpretative possibilities. There is a certain joy in exploring the contradictions, but the overall circumstances have been imposed. Finally, and not insignificantly at all, the butcher's knife rehearsed on a small scale in "A Crossbreed" indeed does terminate Joseph K.'s confusion, suffering, contempt, and despair.

The legacy of "The Cares of a Family Man" is more obviously an artificial construction with implications for the literary artist's deployment of language. Yet it too arrives with a sense of fatality, behaves with humor and absurdity, and relates to the family man with an almost stifling intimacy and familiarity.

> Some say the word Odradek is of Slavonic origin. . . . Others again believe it to be of German origin. . . . The uncertainty of both interpretations allows one to assume with justice that neither is accurate, especially as neither of them provides an intelligent meaning of the word.
>
> No one, of course, would occupy himself with such studies if there were not a creature called Odradek. At first glance it looks like a flat star-shaped spool for thread. . . . But it is not only a spool, for a small wooden crossbar sticks out of the middle of the star, and another small rod is joined to that at a right angle. By means of this latter rod on one side and one of the points of the star on the other, the whole thing can stand upright as if on two legs. (*CS,* 427–28)

The narrative here questions "Odradek's" status both as a name and as a physical collation of incongruous objects. (In this latter respect, Kafka is "sculpting" with words the kind of artwork constructed of things by major modernist sculptors including Picasso, Duchamp, and Moholy-Nagy.) If the crossbreed illustrates the heritage and burden of family life, and its generative role in the motivation of art, Odradek articulates the artist's legacies in cultural and linguistic terms.

If the artist-son's legacy is "not content with being lamb and cat," why need it content itself with being all animate, all inanimate, all human, or all anything? This is what "The Cares of a Family Man" asks. Odradek is precisely an amalgam of fragments. From the history of language it derives its uncertain parentage; from the history of Western religions, its shape (a Christian crossbar fused into a Jewish star); from the world of textiles and threads—always a charged literary image—its broken-off and intertwined substance. Like the kitten/lamb, Odradek sustains incompatible logical conditions. Made of inert things, it stands. Inanimate in nature, it speaks.

> He lurks by turns in the garret, the stairway, the lobbies, the entrance hall. Often for months on end he is not to be seen; then he has presumably moved into other houses; but he always comes faithfully back to our house again. Many a time when you go out of the door and he happens just to be leaning directly beneath you against the banisters you feel inclined to speak to him. Of course, you put no difficult questions to him, you treat him—he is so diminutive that you cannot help it—rather like a child. "Well, what's your name?" you ask him. "Odradek," he says. "And where do you live?" "No fixed abode," he says and laughs; but it is only the kind of laughter that has no lungs behind it. It sounds rather like the rustling of fallen leaves. (CS, 428)

Odradek marks a spot more than he contains an essence or represents an idea. And the spot he marks, the place he occupies, is that of the language which is the literary artist's medium. This is an unsubstantial, shifting place, as exemplified by Odradek's movements in the fable. Just as the kitten/lamb situates itself *between* more than *in* any of the categories it occupies, Odradek resides in the no-man's-land between life and death. The lifeless extreme of Odradek's register endows his own language and activity with a morbid tone, extending into the narrator's collaboration with time.

I ask myself, to no purpose, what is likely to happen to him? Can he possibly die? Anything that dies has had some kind of aim in life, some kind of activity, which has worn out; but that does not apply to Odradek. Am I to suppose, then, that he will always be rolling down the stairs, with ends of thread trailing after him, right before the feet of my children, and my children's children? He does no harm to anyone that one can see; but the idea that he is likely to survive me I find almost painful. (CS, 429)

In this fable, the legacy's autonomy, the art object's capability to exist autonomously from its owner, is viewed as a threat rather than with bemused wonder. The artist-son has been transformed into the resentful and possessive parent of his own work, engaged in a competitive relationship with it. Whether it is the son or the artwork that emerges victorious, the artistic legacy raises the questions of mortality, annihilation, and death. The son is driven to his art by a certain indifferent necessity; and the process of creating artwork both intensifies and ends his suffering. The distance between the vibrant wit that we observe in both parables of inheritance and a morbid resignation to death and suffering—even a solicitation of them—is brief indeed.

But what is the nature of the authority and necessity driving the Kafkan son to despair, suffering, and not least of all, to art? For an answer to this question, we turn to "The Judgment," a story that Kafka considered the turning point of his fictive career when he wrote it during an all-night session on the evening of 22, September 1912. "The Judgment" is the first of his works in which a full-fledged image of the father appears. Among the many achievements of this story may be counted the devastating equilibrium with which Kafka sustains sharply opposed interpretations of reality held by a father and a son, one only intensified by the narrator's shifting loyalties, impossible to "pin down" or ascertain. In a sense, Kafka is treating his readers to two stories for the price of one in this text. In one of them, corresponding to the son's point of view and his basic sense of reality, the son, in the wake of a childhood and youth spent in productive and loyal relationships with his family and friends, has arrived on the threshold of manhood. He has cared for his aging father since the death of his mother two years earlier. "During those two years the [family] business had developed in a most unexpected way, the staff had had to be doubled, the turnover was five times as great; no doubt about it, further progress lay just ahead" (*CS*, 79). This is a stunning record of progress, qualified only by the narrator's interjections, "perhaps . . . due to an unexpected run of good fortune" and the strange assurance, "no doubt about it" (*CS*, 78–79); I will have more on the narrator's secret sharing in this business below. In addition, Georg Bendemann, the son, "had got engaged a month ago to a Fräulein Freida Brandenfeld, a girl from a well-to-do family" (*CS*, 79). This overall picture of fulfillment and success, as Georg experiences it, is compounded by a giving and long-standing relationship he maintains by correspondence with "an old friend of his who was now living abroad" who "was carrying on a business in St. Petersburg" (*CS*, 77). The story's initial dramatic situation, and the medium through which Georg's recent experiences and basic "take" on reality are transmitted to us, consists of a letter he is composing to his friend at the very beginning of the story.

Part of the brilliance of this story resides in the fashion in which it undermines the son's glowing picture of reality (it begins on "a Sunday morning in the very height of spring" [*CS*, 77]) without entirely discounting it. The dramatic climax of "The Judgment" occurs at a moment when Georg, propelled by a sense of well-being, enters his father's darkened bedroom in order to cheer him up and inform him "that I am now sending the news of my engagement to St. Petersburg" (*CS*, 81). In this scene, the rug is literally pulled out from under Georg. His father, who has seemed to have reduced capacities in recent times, appears to him as "still a giant of a man" (*CS*, 81). By the end of this scene, when he will have delivered an unspecified death sentence to Georg, an act of extreme significance for *The Trial*, the senior Bendemann will have thrown his blankets "off with a strength that sent them all flying in a moment and sprang erect in bed" (*CS*, 84), one of the great dramatic reversals in the fictive literature with which I am familiar. Bendemann senior systematically refutes the fundamental assumptions upon which Georg bases his well-being and understanding of reality. " 'Because she lifted up her skirts,' his father began to flute," in reference to Georg's forthcoming marriage and his fiancée,

> "because she lifted her skirts like this, the nasty creature," and mimicking her he lifted his shirt so high that one could see the scar on his thigh from his war wound, "because she lifted her skirts like this and this you made up to her, and in order to make free with her undisturbed you have disgraced your mother's memory, betrayed your friend, and stuck your father into bed so that he can't move. But he can move, or can't he?"
>
> And he stood up quite unsupported and kicked his legs out. His insight made him radiant.
>
> Georg shrank into a corner, as far away from his father as possible. A long time ago he had firmly made up his mind to watch closely every least movement so that he should not be surprised by any indirect attack, a pounce from behind or above. At this moment he recalled this long-forgotten resolve and forgot it again, like a man drawing a short thread through the eye of a needle. (*CS*, 85)

The issue with which "The Judgment" confronts us here is not so much ascertaining which character's view of reality, the son's or the father's, is "true" (although it demands that we consider the question), but rather the coexistence, in a situation of pronounced intimacy, of dramatically opposed points of view. The father's picture of reality is, until the end of the story, a suppressed and silent undercurrent of the son's. The linchpin of the story, the only "objective" element, allowing for the contrapuntal attitudes of father and son to be "tested," is the friend in Russia, the absent correspondent. The interest of this vague interloper on the scene, who bridges past and present, paternal and filial points of view, is represented by neither *present* character but by the implied presence of the narrator. In this regard, the structurally necessary, but for Kafka thoroughly suspect, figure of the narrator becomes the butler in a murder mystery, the anonymous functional figure who somehow holds the key.

In "The Judgment" Kafka explored the full verifying, distorting, and desubstantializing potentials of the narrator for the first time. He will continue this inquest in *The Trial* and in certain other works of short fiction, such as "First Sorrow," discussed below.

"The Judgment" does not resolve the question of whether Georg's fiancée has won him through the crudest of wiles or whether he has somehow sent off his friend to endure failure in Russia. But it does register the son's superior and condescending attitude to his friend, making the father's allegations not entirely untenable. The agent who betrays the secret of the son's contempt, who lets the cat out of the bag, is none other than the narrator, who does this in the least offensive (and punishable) manner possible: by preventing the son's implicit attitudes in a "natural" and transparent way. In the following passage from "The Judgment" it is not Georg who speaks, but rather the narrator who betrays his implicit assumptions.

> What could one write to such a man, who had obviously run off the rails, a man one could be sorry for but could not help. Should one advise him to come home, to transplant himself and take up his old friendships again—there was nothing to hinder him—and in general to rely on the help of his friends? But that was as good as telling him, and the more kindly the more offensively, that all his efforts hitherto had miscarried, that he should finally give up, come back home, and be gaped at by everyone as a returned prodigal, that only his friends knew what was what and that he himself was just a big child who should do what his successful and home-keeping friends prescribed. (*CS*, 77–78)

With these words, the narrative represents Georg's meandering thoughts as he sets about to write his friend a letter. Were we to extract the overall position that these words imply, we might call it the Discourse of the Son, the slightly smug, subtly aggressive sense of superiority with which the son assumes the familial burden of continuity and the transmission of values, mores, and the like. The opposed Discourse of the Father is knowing, skeptical, and thoroughly undeluded. Detached from their characters, these discourses reside at the heart of fiction. They correspond to necessary, but ultimately dispensable, moments of fictive process. The son, in order to work, in order to assume the considerable burden of his patrimony, needs to believe in, if nothing else, himself. The father has survived long enough, has witnessed enough delusory ideologies and calls to action, whether personal or collective, to have deserved, paid for, his unrelenting cynicism. By the same token, the work of fiction constrains the reader to believe and disbelieve, to absorb oneself in the constructed fantasy and then to penetrate its distortions. It is within an allegory of fictive process that the son's self-motivating fantasies of his goodness must be short-lived, must submit to the father's cynicism and judgment, not because they are false but because the wider panorama of fiction ultimately disqualifies all interested points of view.

Is Georg sentenced to death by his father simply for thinking himself superior to his ostensible (he never appears in the story) friend? This would amount to thought crime, punishment for one's ideas alone. But the narrator, that manipulative agent of no loyalty whatsoever, does catch Georg in the act. The narrator, ostensibly playing the role of "objective" reporter, "records" Georg's words to his friend on the subject of his forthcoming marriage.

> And in fact he did inform his friend, in the long letter. . . . "I have got engaged to a Fräulein Frieda Brandenfeld, a girl from a well-to-do family, who only came to live here a long time after you went away, so that you're hardly likely to know her. . . . I know that there are many reasons why you can't come to see us, but would not my wedding be precisely the right occasion for giving all obstacles the go-by? Still, however that may be, do just as seems good to you without regarding any interests but your own."
>
> With this letter in his hand Georg had been sitting a long time at the writing table, his face turned toward the window. (*CS*, 80)

No passage in the story better typifies the combination of good will and resentment that could characterize the son's position. The son does feel a genuine warmth for the correspondent at the same time that he assures him, "you will acquire in my fiancée, who sends her warm greetings and will soon write you herself, a genuine friend of the opposite sex." Kafka has achieved here, in fictive discourse, the difficult task of representing a consciousness at least in part hidden from itself, divided, in the terms of depth psychology, along the vertical split separating calm and grandiose self-fragments.

The son *writes out* the superior sense of himself that he uses in order to motivate himself to assume his considerable interpersonal and professional burden. He thus concretizes the positions that his father, with a survivor's healthy cynicism, will be able to debunk, one by one. Herein consists the offense on the basis of which the father sentences him "now to death by drowning!" (*CS*, 87). In death, Georg holds as resolutely to his filial piety as his father does to his self-righteous cynicism: "With weakening grip he was still holding on when he spied between the railings a motor-bus coming which would easily cover the noise of his fall, called in a low voice: 'Dear parents, I have always loved you, all the same,' and let himself drop" (*CS*, 88). Even in dying, Georg retains a certain shame at the inconvenience his death will cause. This is not unlike the brother's concern, in "The Knock at the Manor Gate," for his sister's dress and modesty. As will become quite apparent in *The Trial,* the Kafkan son's sensibility vacillates in an important way between contempt and shame.

In a story that Kafka considered a turning point in his career, a son estranged from his father and his obligations writes a revealing letter and dies a "larger than life" death. (He "felt himself urged" from the room where his father condemned him, out of the apartment, and toward the bridge to which he clings for one final moment [*CS*, 87–88]). "The Judgment" may well be the fullest elaboration of the familial compulsion at the basis of art in Kafka's fiction, a tale in which familial tension and ambivalence are superbly translated into narrative complexity. We will want to bear in mind the questionable loyalty of its narrator and its association of writing with guilt, suffering, and death as we read *The Trial*.

In such works as "First Sorrow" and "A Hunger Artist" the generational battle between father and son in "The Judgment" is transformed into artistic conflict between the idealism, or rather extremism, of the artist and the practicality advocated by his handlers or managers. These latter figures are men whose services to the artists they represent are vaguely suggestive of a paternal bearing. Hermann Kafka's business career cannot be entirely irrelevant here. In such works as "First Sorrow" and "A Hunger Artist," in other words, conflicts elsewhere situated within the familial domain (for example, "The Judgment" and "The Metamorphosis") have been translated into the terms, settings, and choices surrounding artistic performance, production, and endurance. These works thus complete a transformation of personal and familial concerns in Kafka's writing into aesthetic ones, although an aura and environment of martyrdom persists throughout their respective dramas. I thus conclude my overview of Kafka's rehearsals to *The Trial* with a brief discussion of them.

The managers of "First Sorrow" and "A Hunger Artist" have evolved from menacing, mediatory father-figures, to artistic facilitators suspicious, if for anything, for their extreme solicitude. Yet, it is possible, as the phrase goes, to kill with kindness. In Kafka's fully realized artistic parables, the manager thwarts the artist-son not with aggression but with exaggerated, ultimately unempathetic, concern, interest in the trappings rather than in the generativity of art. The artist-son's medium in "First Sorrow," an allegory whose achievement is in no way diminished by its brevity, is, significantly, trapeze artistry, an art form literally dramatizing the superiority of art over the mundane concerns of everyday life, art's suspension of the most basic laws and limits.

> A trapeze artist . . . never came down from his trapeze by night or day, at first only from a desire to perfect his skill, but later because custom was too strong for him. All his needs, very modest needs at that, were supplied by relays of attendants who watched from below. . . . Yet the management overlooked this, because he was an extraordinary and unique artist. And of course they recognized that this mode of life was no mere prank, and that only in this way could he really keep himself in constant practice and his art at the pitch of its perfection. (*CS*, 446)

This paragraph, the first of "First Sorrow," is informed by two vital tensions, related to one another in important ways: between the "above" and the "below" of the artistic performance (respectively, where it takes place and where it is fostered) and between the text's mannerisms and the substance of what it reports. Time, for this artist at least, is better spent in the stratosphere of his calling. The elevation of his métier and his location increasingly captivates and confines him. His inclination to physically sublimate himself causes him "no particular inconvenience" because his needs are "very modest needs at that." The trapeze artist's unique attitude, motivated by a certain revulsion at the world of concrete concerns, does require, on the other hand, unusual and extreme efforts on the part of those in his entourage. Here once again, the narrative voice deviates from its all too easily assumed fidelity to the events and the truth. For the narrative voice, in this passage, records the extraordinary events necessary to keep the trapeze artist aloft without any reference to their cost; it suppresses the effect of the artist's possibly immoderate demand; it insinuates, in other words, the artist's tunnel vision into its ostensibly objective report to the audience; it participates in a rationalization of the artist's demand at the level of narrative reportage. From the beginning, where it assures us that trapeze artistry is one of "the most difficult humanity can achieve," the narrative voice relinquishes any disinterest we might assume would constrain it, and initiates a program of whitewashing and suppressing the anger, distrust, and contempt implicit in the artist's demand. It assures us of the modesty of his needs and the mere inconvenience they cause his handlers, and it informs us that "he was an extraordinary and unique artist," thus justifying any extraordinary measures undertaken on his behalf.

The narrative voice thus steps into the role of an overindulgent parent in respect to the artist. The most fundamental psychology teaches us that such exaggerated empathy is as much an aggression, contains as much the wish to stifle and defeat the child, as more explicit forms of opposition. It does this while performing a function that the most overly finicky reader might still assume to be neutral. In other words, the narrative suppresses, masks, its aggression to itself; its aggression is thus acted out not only toward the touchy artist but also toward the reader. As the tale proceeds, the overprotective measures that the manager undertakes on the artist's behalf only proliferate.

> The trapeze artist could have gone on living peacefully like that, had it not been for the inevitable journeys from place to place, which he found extremely trying. Of course his manager saw to it

that his sufferings were not prolonged one moment more than necessary; for town travel, racing automobiles were used, which whirled him, by night if possible or in the earliest hours of the morning, through the empty streets at breakneck speed, too slow all the same for the trapeze artist's impatience; for railway journeys, a whole compartment was reserved, in which the trapeze artist, as a possible though wretched alternative to his usual way of living, could pass the time up on the luggage rack; in the next town on their circuit, long before he arrived, the trapeze was already slung up in the theater and all the doors leading to the stage were flung wide open, all corridors kept free—yet the manager never knew a happy moment until the trapeze artist set his foot on the rope ladder and in a twinkling, at long last, hung aloft on his trapeze. (*CS*, 447)

Here Kafka's catalogue of managerial arrangements extends well into the hilarious. But their extremity should not suppress the fact that the manager and the narrator assume parallel functions. Both usurp manipulative control through the deflection of legitimate concerns. The manager reassures the artist that his demands are all right, while the narrator assures us that the artist's character is a natural outgrowth of artistry and aesthetics. The manager gradually assumes the protective, naturalizing, self-deceiving function in relation to the trapeze artist that the narrator first rehearsed to the reader. The end consequence of such narrative phrases as "very modest needs at that" (*CS*, 446), "this mode of life was no mere prank" (*CS*, 446), and "Besides, it was quite healthful up there" (*CS*, 446) are such arrangements as the racing cars, reserved railroad compartments, and hanging in a luggage rack, by which the manager assures the artist's insulation from the mundane and distressing. The artist and his impresario perfectly mirror one another in another sense: the manager's practical expertise, his savoir faire, fully measures up to this "extraordinary and unique artist." While the artist, with some considerable degree of revulsion, resists the constraints of circumstances and practicality, and even the fundamental laws governing such phenomena as time, space, and gravity, the manager, with his own brand of ingenuity and success, negotiates all sorts of pressing logistical demands.

There is greater equality between the brilliant artist and his practical handler than might meet the eye, just as Hermann Kafka might have been, at least in psychological terms, a more formidable interlocutor to his son Franz than the record indicates. Where "First Sorrow" explores the meaningful interaction between these two characters, it shifts its allegory from logistical to literary terms. It emerges, as the story develops, that the artist is a dreamer and the impresario a reader, the artist a communicator of disturbing images and thoughts, the impresario an interpreter of his gestures and messages. The two figures only not share a business interest, with its various bottom lines, but also an allegory and a dynamic of reading and writing.

> Once when they were again traveling together . . . the trapeze artist addressed his companion in a low voice. The manager was immediately all attention. The trapeze artist, biting his lips, said that he must always in future have two trapezes for his performance instead of only one, two trapezes opposite each other. The manager at once agreed. But the trapeze artist, as if to show that the manager's consent counted for as little as his refusal, said that never again would he perform on only one trapeze. . . . The very idea that it might happen at all seemed to make him shudder. The manager, watchfully feeling his way, once more emphasized his entire agreement. . . . At that the trapeze artist suddenly burst into tears. Deeply distressed, the manager sprang to his feet and asked what was the matter, then getting no answer climbed up on the seat and caressed him, cheek to cheek, so that his own face was bedabbled by the trapeze artist's tears. . . . The trapeze artist sobbed: "Only the one bar in my hands—how can I go on living!" That made it somewhat easier for the manager to comfort him; he promised to wire from the very next station for a second trapeze to be installed in the first town on their circuit; reproached himself for having let the artist work so long on only one trapeze. . . . And so he succeeded in reassuring the trapeze artist, little by little. . . . But he himself was far from reassured. (CS, 447–48)

The dramatic climax of this existential and aesthetic tragedy disarmingly disguised as a fable or modern-day fairy tale occurs when the artist's incessant demands to surpass the limits of reality exceed the impresario's demonstrated capabilities, thus rupturing the perfect sympathy between the two characters. This passage marks several crucial transitions: for example, of the artist's compulsions from possibility to impossibility, and of the impresario's ministrations from sufficiency to insufficiency. The most important development that the passage marks, however, is the necessity for the frustration of desire to be registered in writing. It is the above passage that allows "First Sorrow" to serve in extreme miniature as a genealogy of Kafka's writing. The tale ends with a sense of ominous and pained anticipation constituting the affective substance of anxiety.

Among the many important details to be noted in the above passage are the following: the symmetry in which the artist and his manager first arrange themselves; the artist's new wish as a logical and spatial *extension* of his given location *above* the ground of everyday concerns; the artist's discomfort over the continuation of his existing conditions ("The very idea . . . seemed to make him shudder"); the intensity and immediacy of the manager's responses to him ("The manager at once agreed. . . . Deeply distressed, the manager sprang to his feet"); and the continuation of the latter's defensive and rationalizing functions ("once more emphasized his entire agreement, two trapezes were better than one, besides it would be an advantage to have a second bar"). The first unresolvable, incorrigible rupture to the mutually dependent, symbiotic relationship between the artist and the impresario results in a "deep concern" on the part of the latter. "The first furrows of care engraving themselves upon the trapeze artist's smooth, childlike forehead" (*CS,* 448) may be interpreted as the translation of unhealed wounds and unsatisfied desires into writing, the birth of the literary artist's art out of his particular, nontransferable pain.

Although the oppositional adversity of "The Judgment" continues into "First Sorrow," the figure of the son has been metamorphosed into an artist, and the father has emerged as a vital, if untrustworthy, partner in the enterprise. The artist-impresario partnership in this text is extremely recognizable to readers of "A Hunger Artist," where the former son's final emanation is as an exhausted and misunderstood martyr. A comprehensive interpretation of this last story is beyond the scope of the present introduction to *The Trial,* but several selected passages will demonstrate, I believe forcefully, the completion of a trinity consisting of the parallel function of a son, an artist, and a martyr whose interplay informs, structures, and occupies thematically much of Kafka's future work, including our subject.

It is finally in "A Hunger Artist" that an artist, whose thin, diminutive body gives him the scale of a son, develops fully into a martyr, rehearsing in miniature the scenario of *The Trial*. Like the gymnastics of the trapeze, public fasting, which was in fact on display in the nineteenth-century circus, is an art assuming the form of *negation*. While the trapeze performer resists the most ineluctable physical laws of gravity and space, the hunger artist demonstrates mastery over the most fundamental laws and desires. A negative relation prevails between this art form and the optimal conditions of life as common sense would translate them, in terms of comfort, well-being, and even health. The *perfection* of this art consists in the denial, reduction, and agony of the body, at least as people with healthy appetites would experience its enforced hunger. This story, structured like *The Trial*, culminates in a paradox, a timeless aphorism that reinforces rather than resolves a tragic stalemate. "Because I couldn't find the food I liked," whispers the emaciated hunger artist with his dying breath in explanation for his métier. "If I had found it, believe me, I should have made no fuss and stuffed myself like you or anyone else" (*CS*, 277). This artist resides very much in the same world as the rest of us. He merely hungers with a different kind of appetite. His food is our hunger; our hunger his food. He whispers with the raspy, nearly inaudible voice of Odradek. In dying, his lips, the same ones he would minimally moisten at the beginning of the story, are "pursed, as if for a kiss" (*CS*, 277), an ultimate pathos.

> During these last decades the interest in professional fasting has markedly diminished. . . . We live in a different world now. At one time the whole town took a lively interest in the hunger artist; from day to day of his fast the excitement mounted; everybody wanted to see him at least once a day; there were people who bought season tickets for the last few days and sat from morning till night in front of his small barred cage; even in the

nighttime there were visiting hours, when the whole effect was heightened by torch flares; on fine days the cage was set out in the open air, and then it was the children's special treat to see the hunger artist; for their elders he was often just a joke that happened to be in fashion, but the children stood openmouthed, holding each other's hands for greater security, marveling at him as he sat there pallid in black tights, with his ribs sticking out so prominently. (*CS,* 268)

Thus begins "A Hunger Artist," written in February 1922, only two and one-third years before Kafka died, a story benefiting from much of what its author had taught himself about fiction. Noteworthy in the above story are its firm historical framework, as opposed to the timelessness of many of the brief parables and even such a realistic story as "The Judgment"; the spatial compartmentalization of the artist in a cage; and the exaggerated modesty and control of his needs, wants, gestures, and in general, his will. While the artist's separation from the rest of humanity in "First Sorrow" was above all an imaginary one, in "A Hunger Artist" the solitude-imposing barrier is concrete, or rather steel. At the same time that the story's historical dimension records the demise of an art form, the physical location of the artist and his cage moves to increasingly remote outposts of the spectacle. While the artist balks at finding any food he can eat, the audience loses its appetite for the entire performance, preferring in the end to revel in a panther's easy sensuality and satisfaction of its hunger.

The hunger artist is a study in denial and self-control. His gestures are courteous; his smiles are constrained; his ribs protrude, but only through the absence of flesh on his body. He does not drink water but grudgingly accepts meager sips from himself. What he demands—his true hunger—is not adulation for his feat but attentiveness and respect from his watchers. The purpose of hunger artistry, as the artist of our story practices it, is not to attenuate the audience's physical discomfort but its intellectual sensibility. It would be easy to overlook in the story's nutritional allegory the fact that the artist, in order to keep his audience awake, in order to transfer the relentlessness of his physical endurance to its sensibility, is also a storyteller, a practitioner of narrative art.

> Much more to his taste were the watchers who sat close up to the bars, who were not content with the dim night lighting of the hall but focused him in the full glare of the electric pocket torch given them by the impresario. The harsh light did not trouble him at all, in any case he could never sleep properly, and he could always drowse a little, whatever the light, at any hour, even when the hall was thronged with noisy onlookers. He was quite happy at the prospect of spending a sleepless night with such watchers; he was ready to exchange jokes with them, to tell them stories out of his nomadic life, anything at all to keep them awake and demonstrate to them again that he had no eatables in his cage and that he was fasting as not one of them could fast. But his happiest moment was when the morning came and an enormous breakfast was brought them, at his expense, on which they flung themselves with the keen appetite of healthy men after a weary night of wakefulness. (CS, 269)

The hunger artist not only entertains his preferred clientele—those who share rather than deny or reduce the aggravated tension aroused by his art—with stories; he delights in the satisfaction of their physical needs. The hunger artist may be said to satisfy his appetite vicariously, through the nourishment of those who can appreciate the denial and displacement that his art demands.

The hunger artist's conflicts are above all with those who are unsympathetic to his striving, his self-sacrifice, and his creativity; with those who, often in the guise of compassion and support, strive to stifle his inevitable calling. These include the watchers who flag in their scrutiny of his feat, "obviously intending to give the hunger artist the chance of a little refreshment" (CS, 269), and his manager, whose scientific knowledge of hunger artistry's audience and duration betrays the venality of his interest in it:

> The longest period of fasting was fixed by his impresario at forty days, beyond that term he was not allowed to go, not even in

great cities, and there was good reason for it, too. Experience had proved that for about forty days the interest of the public could be stimulated by a steadily increasing pressure of advertisement, but after that the town began to lose interest, sympathetic support began notably to fall off. . . . So on the fortieth day the flower-bedecked cage was opened, enthusiastic spectators filled the hall, a military band played, two doctors entered the cage to measure the results of the fast, which were announced through a mega-phone, and finally two young ladies appeared, blissful at having been selected for the honor, to help the hunger artist down the few steps leading to a small table on which was spread a carefully chosen invalid repast. And at this very moment the artist always turned stubborn. . . . Why stop now, when he was in his best fast-ing form, or rather, not yet quite in his best fasting form? (*CS*, 270–71)

Nowhere in Kafka's writing does the hypocrisy surrounding the artistic performance emerge with greater force or clarity. While the very nature of this art form is to suspend or attenuate itself, as in the case of trapeze artistry, the concerns of practicality, as implemented by the impresario and the curious "ladies," militate against its completion. The scenario of artistic production in the above passage is one of con-tempt disguised as adulation. The father of "The Judgment" has learned a certain tact befitting his good business sense, but he still opposes and resists the son's unique talents and artistic sensitivities.

The instruments deployed by management to rein the artist in, however, are women. Kafka plays on societal expectations of feminine passivity and restraint to emphasize the contrast between the ladies' exaggerated concern and their repressive effect upon the artistic per-formance. The hunger artist's gaze "into the eyes of the ladies who were apparently so friendly and in reality so cruel" as the impresario cuts short his performance (*CS*, 271) continues a tradition of ambiva-lence toward heterosexuality that Kafka registers in his *Diaries*[3] and that we will confront in the alternation between the lively Fräulein Bürstner and her sickly substitute, Fräulein Montag, at the beginning of *The Trial*—and in Joseph K.'s participation in a homoerotically charged whipping scene in chapter 5 of the novel.

Hunger artistry shares the logic of potentially endless extension that Kafka associated with the aesthetic sensibility since early in his experiments. "Not content with being lamb and cat, it [the crossbreed] almost insists on being a dog as well" (CS, 427). Yet the central poignancy of the hunger artist's tale is not so much his progressive exile from the limelight and his marginalization, but the hypocrisy and lack of sympathy with which key figures (his manager and "ladies" in general) greet his art. Composition of "A Hunger Artist" coincided with the beginning of Kafka's third and final novel, The Castle, in which Kafka conjured up his fullest and culminating vision of indifference and unresponsiveness. In this novel, the Castle administration responds to the protagonist's (now known as K.) efforts to secure social and economic acceptance with a disregard so blunt as often to be humorous.

This kind of misunderstanding and indifference are far more draining to the hunger artist than his singular dietary habits. He dies a martyr—to misinterpretation and the lack of empathy—more than because his placards have failed and because he has been moved to the hinterlands of the sideshow. The hunger artist suffers a martyrdom of oblivion. He is located by circus attendants poking around his pallet. In death, he holds on to "the firm though no longer proud persuasion that he was continuing to fast" (CS, 277), just as Georg Bendemann, at the end of "The Judgment," futilely holds fast to the bridge of human language and communication and his dutiful love for his parents.

The backdrop against which I have framed The Trial, extending from some of Kafka's earlier experiments to a great story concurrent with his final novel, has not exactly followed a straight and narrow route. But it does indicate, I think, the profundity and rigor with which Kafka undertook parallel meditations into his status: as the son of his particular family and times, as an individual who thought through his existential and intellectual problems in a process of literary creativity, and as a person who, artistically and on an imaginary level, suffered considerable familial conflict, self-doubt, isolation, and loneliness.

Kafka's enormous influence and popularity as an author are related to readers' abilities to identify with his imagery and the sociopsychological situations in which his characters find themselves. Like many of today's students in Europe and America, Kafka belonged to the generation immediately following his family's first rise above the ground-level of basic material concerns. He benefited from the education, wherewithall, and leisure time to observe his family and society and their wider historical circumstances with considerable critical detachment. While his health permitted, he could respond to developments in technology, fashion, leisure, and other social phenomena with the same amusement, wonder, and occasional horror dawning upon other young adults during their formative educational and maturational years. (Kafka was diagnosed as having tuberculosis in 1917, and during the last four years of his life the disease increasingly sapped his energies.) Kafka's writing in general and *The Trial* in particular are compelling because Kafka was an exceptionally inventive citizen of his times, culture, and literary tradition. He anticipated several of his times' most original and characteristic literary inventions: a simultaneous observation through several different perspectives that I have elsewhere described as superimposition[4]; an extended literary rumination whose underlying characteristics, like trapeze and hunger artistries, seem to be its suspension and proliferation; a composition of literary hybrids, such as Odradek, out of his culture's discarded odds and ends.

Although Kafka concocted situations, characters, and creatures of striking oddity, his fiction rings with uncanny psychological verisimilitude. To this catalogue of his contributions I would like to add his remarkable anticipation of the conditions of subjectivity in late-capitalist and totalitarian societies during the twentieth century. Whether we choose to explain this subjectivity in terms of psychological repression and blocked drives, as Freud did, or in terms of borderline phenomena first noted in fiction by Viennese novelist Robert Musil and by later psychoanalysts such as Heinz Kohut and Otto Kernberg, Kafka's fiction resonates with issues of false self and subjective emptiness. Among Kafka's most enduring contributions was his work as a prophet and critic of subjective conditions; citizens of late-capitalist societies are still working through an alternation between grandiose and degraded states of mind, a gravitation toward the borderline of acceptable interpersonal relations.

Oppressed yet inspired by his own legacies, Kafka left a literary inheritance, including *The Trial,* whose flowering and generativity continue.

5

A Courthouse of Codes and Messages

The initial chapter of *The Trial* is important not only because it inaugurates one of the twentieth century's most innovative and characteristic novels but because it introduces the images, codes, and themes within whose purview the novel's most important developments take place. *The Trial* is as much about changes within certain attitudes and perspectives as it is about the events of Joseph K.'s life and death.

I will gloss this chapter carefully, because the "files" it opens continue through the novel. My model for reading chapter 1 of *The Trial* will be the method that the French critic Roland Barthes created in his book *S/Z* for interpreting "Sarrazine," a short story by Honoré de Balzac.[1] In *S/Z*, Barthes analyzes "Sarrazine" into its semiological codes, according to certain umbrellas or rubrics under which certain of its most telling signs fall. Barthes was a mid-century master of semiology, the study of artistic and cultural artifacts according to the sign systems of which they are made and the manner in which their particular signs, symbols, images, and words function. *The Trial*, like any densely worded artifact of language, can be regarded as the product and intersection of the respective sign systems comprising it. Although I will reference slightly different categories than Barthes did in reading "Sarrazine," I will interpret *The Trial*'s first chapter by ask-ing which types of codes Kafka involves in composing his text and how they operate together.

The concurrent perspectives of son, artist, and martyr through which the Kafkan protagonist experiences and interprets the world continue to influence the novel profoundly when it is analyzed in terms of its prevailing codes, images, and formal devices. The novel articulates the perspective of the son to the degree that it is concerned with childhood, tradition, and the literary conventions and fragments out of which it is fashioned. The novel deliberately leaves us in the dark about much of this information as it concerns Joseph K. This informational blackout adds to the ominousness of the Court and its proceedings; it is a device that Kafka also uses in such works as "In the Penal Colony" and *The Castle*. At the same time, *The Trial* presents glimmerings about Joseph K.'s status as a son. In the Court offices, he discovers the Examining Magistrate's pornography collection; a seedy sex life opens up in a figure of paternal authority. He is very much a nephew in the novel if not explicitly a son. His Uncle Karl tries to take the matter of his trial in hand, and leads him to the apartment of Lawyer Huld, but Joseph K. devotes his attentions to Huld's nurse Leni rather than to his advocate's best advice. (Uncles, including Alfred Löwy, director of a Spanish railroad, Siegfried Löwy, a "country doc-tor," and bookkeeper Rudolf Löwy, a confirmed bachelor, happened to play an important role in the education of Franz Kafka.) Finally, an interest in childhood experience and memories parallel to Proust's, beginning with "Children on a Country Road," runs throughout Kafka's fiction. The children that Joseph K. encounters in Court painter Titorelli's building belong very much to this strain in Kafka's work, one in which the protagonist and children often function side by side as prior and subsequent versions of one another.

Joseph K. meets a practicing artist in the course of the novel, who explains the varieties of uncertainty his trial has injected into his life. The aesthetic dimension of his experience is registered both in the complexities he addresses and in the novel's distinctive style and for-mal innovations. It is of great moment to the novel, for example, whether its chapters, like the first, "The Arrest, Conversation with

Frau Grubach, Then Fräulein Bürstner," are complex in structure, extending to several episodes, which gives them an exhausting quality, or whether they focus, like chapter 5, "The Whipper," on one sharply delineated scene. The alternation between concentrated and diffuse units in the novel comprises one further instance of Kafka's exploration of the fictive potentials and liabilities in the fragment and the whole. The narrative function in *The Trial*, like that of "The Judgment," is not always aboveboard or crystal clear in its allegiances. Both Joseph K. and the reader experience his appearances before the Examining Magistrate and other Court officials as performances. The reader shares with Joseph K. the outbreaks of dizziness and temporal and spatial disorientation that overcome him in the Court offices and at the bank where he works. At Lawyer Huld's apartment, in Titorelli's atelier, and in the Cathedral where Joseph K. hears the Parable of the Doorkeeper and its elucidation, he happens upon portraits, painted representations framed by the novel as well as by their physical homes. These portraits draw attention to and comment upon the novel's own artificial devices. In all the above ways and more, the novel registers, dramatizes, and elucidates the sensibility of a certain kind of artist and aesthetic theory.

Whether we understand how or why—and the novel posits its own suggestions—Joseph K. has broken the Law. To the degree that *The Trial* opens up a setting of law, authority, mythology, and theology in which Joseph K. functions antagonistically, it records his role as a martyr. The novel does not take long to tell us that Joseph K. is doomed. We should see this clearly in the second chapter if we have not intuited it in the first, where his arrest is a foregone conclusion. The inevitable death of a character whose common sense, petty egotism, and predictable desires make him so much a reflection of ourselves evokes the pathos and empathy whose original vehicle was classical tragedy. The novel provides ample evidence that Joseph K.'s "real" crime, for which he must suffer public humiliation and the losses of his work and life, is nothing more serious than falling in and out of a prideful contempt for his fellows and their surroundings. This vacillation between contempt and shame is the stuff personality disorders (as opposed to the structural Freudian neuroses) are made of. The punishment he suffers for his quirks, his at-worst symbolic sins, is an extreme one, but it brings the theme of martyrdom in Kafka's work to the magnificent culmination formulated in the Parable of the Doorkeeper (in chapter 9).

The Trial, then, is the intersection of its own images, codes, and formal devices, and Kafka's long-standing philosophical and artistic bearings. We will be examining certain of its pivotal passages closely. There is no better place to inaugurate such an undertaking than the very beginning of the text. The first narrative unit of *The Trial* is one of its composite, hybrid chapters consisting of multiple episodes (in this case three), each remarkable for its compression. The chapter begins with a narration of Joseph K.'s arrest one morning just after he has awakened and of the arbitrariness this legal incident introduces into his life (*T*, 1–17), pauses over a conversation between him and Frau Grubach, his landlady, whose somewhat prosaic normality contrasts with her ability to accept the absurdity of her tenant's arrest (*T*, 17–22), and ends with an encounter between the suspect and Fräulein Bürstner, his single "sexually eligible" counterpart in the domestic arrangement. These episodes interlock in a complex way. They lead in and out of each other like the rooms in a convoluted apartment, or like the offices of a Court extending, in relentless and possible malevolent fashion, to every kind of residential and personal space and type of neighborhood (or like the architecture of the Castle in Kafka's final novel). In their structural complexity, such amalgamated chapters as 1, 3, 6, 7, and 8, themselves composed of condensed fragmentary scenes and playing with the notion of the fragment, approximate the narrative equivalent of a bewildering, impacted, and sometimes repetitive architecture.

Chapter 1, whose first sentence we have already studied, begins in the following way:

> Someone must have been telling lies about Joseph K., for without having done anything wrong he was arrested one fine morning. His landlady's cook, who always brought him his breakfast at eight o'clock, failed to appear on this occasion. That had never

happened before. K. waited for a little while longer, watching from his pillow the old lady opposite, who seemed to be peering at him with a curiosity unusual even for her, but then, feeling both put out and hungry, he rang the bell. (*T*, 1)

TONE

As suggested above, ominous, threat assuming the form of indefiniteness: "Someone must have been telling lies." What is known here, "he was arrested one fine day," is known only indirectly, by inference. The tone in these lines is even and distant throughout, and although their subject matter changes somewhat drastically, the tone remains one of matter-of-fact detachment.

NARRATOR

It is the narrator who informs us that the morning is "fine" and, more importantly, that Joseph K. has done nothing wrong. The narrative function camouflages the leverage it exerts on the reportage in its seemingly objective tone. As "The Judgment" also suggests, "without having done anything wrong" Joseph K. is nonetheless quite capable of feeling wrong, in bad faith, of quite genuinely participating in a dynamic of self-righteousness, guilt, and shame.

SETTING

Normality, everydayness. To achieve its dramatic impact, Joseph K.'s arrest must collide at full speed with the ritual and ambiance of custom. The personification of custom in this case is the "landlady's cook, who always brought him his breakfast at eight o'clock" and who "failed to appear on this occasion." The Court has already penetrated into the bastion of Joseph K.'s private life, his landlady's apartment. As we shall see in the lines below, this invasion is not the least of its achievements and shows of force.

MODE ?

The unusual, the unprecedented: "That had never happened before."

AFFECT

On the part of Joseph K. as well as the old lady "opposite" (across the hall? the street?), curiosity, slight annoyance, "feeling both put out and hungry."

GENRE

Theater. The old lady comprises the first in a series of audiences that will include some of Joseph K.'s neighbors and those assisting at his Sunday interrogation. It may be said that Joseph K.'s actions and even thoughts in *The Trial* seldom take place far from an audience that Kafka internalizes into the novel. In this sense, as James Rolleston has argued, *The Trial* is truly a theatrical novel although it also communicates in interesting ways with tragedies, holy scripture, satires, and allegories.[2] The presence and influence of an internal audience within the scenario become only more interesting when Kafka neglects to depict one. Joseph K. rarely steps outside a theatrical scene; he always plays before the audience of Kafka's readers, whether or not in a given scene Kafka chooses to incorporate a surrogate audience as well.

> At once there was a knock at the door and a man entered whom he had never seen before in the house. He was slim and yet well knit, he wore a closely fitting black suit furnished with all sorts of

pleats, pockets, buckles, and buttons, as well as a belt, like a tourist's outfit, and in consequence looked eminently practical, though one could not quite tell what actual purpose it served. "Who are you?" asked K., half raising himself in bed. But the man ignored the question, as though his appearance needed no explanation, and merely said: "Did you ring?" "Anna is to bring me my breakfast," said K., and then studied the fellow, silently and carefully, trying to make out who he could be. The man did not submit to this scrutiny for very long, but turned to the door and opened it slightly so as to report to someone who was evidently standing just behind it: "He says Anna is to bring him his breakfast." A short guffaw from the next room came in answer; and it rather sounded as if several people had joined in. Although the strange man could not have learned anything from it that he did not know already, he now said to K., as if passing on a statement: "It can't be done." (*T*, 1–2)

TENOR OF EVENTS

Suddenness, precipitousness: "At once there was a knock . . . and a man entered."

SEXUALITY

"He was slim and well built." No doubt about it, Kafka's fiction is as receptive to male beauty and female disfiguration, which do not necessarily proceed from each other, as it is to their opposites. The climax to the novel's homoerotic conflict occurs during the sadomasochistic whipping scene in chapter 5. Of the novel's possible sexual counterparts to Joseph K., only Fräulein Bürstner of the first chapter is presented as physically unscathed. Fräulein Montag, her replacement in the apartment, is described as "a sickly, pale girl with a slight limp" (*T*, 75). Between the two middle fingers of her right hand, Leni, Lawyer Huld's nurse, has a "connecting web of skin" reaching "almost to the top joint, short as the fingers were" (*T*, 110), a disfiguration that her cinematographic substitute, Romy Schneider (in Orson Welles's 1962 *The Trial*) displays to its full uncanny advantage.

CODE

Clothing. Like Joyce, Kafka is unusually sensitive to his characters' coverings. He delights in precise descriptions of uniforms: Warder Franz's in this passage; the Court usher's buttons (*T*, 165); Mr. Samsa's bank messenger's uniform in "The Metamorphosis" (*CS*, 121, 123); and the suits worn by different levels of village and castle officials in *The Castle*.

MODES

Humor, absurdity. The uniform worn by the Court warder interestingly named Franz is a wonder of obsessive details, marvelously out of place in a beginning so otherwise ominous. Here we can posit one meaning (out of many possibilities) of the term "Kafkaesque": the jarring, unannounced juxtaposition, akin to the Freudian condensation, of moods. In this passage, Kafka passes almost without notice from dark foreboding to satiric mockery, an attitude that Franz himself assumes when he reports Joseph K.'s desire for his breakfast from Anna to his cohorts in the adjoining room.

SOCIAL ALLEGORY

Societal indifference, authoritarianism. In judgmental fashion, Franz declares that Joseph K.'s customary life is now beyond the realm of possibility. Among Franz's tasks is confining Joseph K. to his own room, an activity all the more repressive in light of the doorkeeper's revelation, in the pivotal Parable, "No one but you could gain admittance through this door, since this door was intended for you" (*T*, 214–15).

Textual Performance

Expansion, proliferation. Our brief fascination with Franz's uniform is indicative of the fashion with which the Court and Law will dominate, in part, through internal complications and elaborations. In *The Trial*, Kafka continues the practice of arresting his readers with scenes of expanding wonder and complexity that he developed in his first novel, the one that came to be known as *Amerika*. Franz's uniform, to be followed in *The Trial* by the descriptions of the Court offices, officers, (*T*, 63, 67–68, 119, 164), and the Law itself (*T*, 213–21), is in the tradition of traffic and telephone systems and a political rally upon which Kafka marvelously elaborated in *Amerika*.

> "This is news indeed," cried K., springing out of bed and quickly pulling on his trousers. "I must see what people these are next door, and how Frau Grubach can account to me for such behavior." Yet it occurred to him at once that he should not have said this aloud and that by doing so he had in a way admitted the stranger's right to superintend his actions; still, that did not seem important to him at the moment. The stranger, however, took his words in some such sense, for he asked: "Hadn't you better stay here?" "I shall neither stay here nor let you address me until you have introduced yourself." "I meant well enough," said the stranger, and then of his own accord threw the door open. In the next room, which K. entered more slowly than he had intended . . . a man . . . was sitting at the open window reading a book, from which he now glanced up. "You should have stayed in your room! Didn't Franz tell you that?" "Yes, but what are you doing here?" asked K., looking from his new acquaintance to the man called Franz, who was still standing by the door, and then back again. (*T*, 2–3)

AFFECT

Indignation in the face of unprovoked aggression and irrationality. Joseph K.'s reactions to the strange turn of events that has intruded upon his life are predictable and, in an everyday sense, reasonable. In his thoughts he appeals to his landlady as an authority in the realm of the everyday, and to the intruders he insists on a politeness ultimately proving futile: "until you have introduced yourself." These are his instinctive defensive reactions to the absurd situation.

PSYCHOLOGICAL STATE

Self-consciousness. In its infantile stages, the affair makes Joseph K. internally aware of his own thoughts and reactions. This heightened self-awareness is akin to the "split" or doubled consciousness that Freud early on associated with several neurotic conditions.[3] In this passage Joseph K. becomes painfully attentive to what he should and should not say, a sensitivity surely appealing to many readers. He joins, in this regard, Melville's Ishmael, Dostoyevski's Raskolnikov and Underground Man, the narrators of such Poe tales as "The Murders in the Rue Morgue," "The Pit and the Pendulum," and "The Tell-tale Heart," and Camus's Meursault as fictive surrogates in which readers have, to an unusual degree, caught a glimpse of their own heightened (or blocked, in the case of Meursault) attentiveness under certain conditions.

MODE

A sudden and violent intrusion upon the most everyday, akin to the Freudian notion of uncanniness. This is the place for the enumeration of the familiar details in Frau Grubach's living arrangements: "furniture, rugs, china, and photographs," an inventory that will be repeated with respect to the objects in Fräulein Bürstner's room. Kafka accentuates the arbitrariness of the intrusion that Joseph K. addresses through the sense of realism he achieves with such details. In the context of Frau Grubach's china and personal photographs, Willem's pronouncement, "You should have stayed in your room!," sounds particularly jarring.

GENRE

Theater of the absurd. The assistance of a senile old biddy at the increasingly extraordinary scene adds one further index or dimension to its unreality.

Quoting liberally from the text, I have attempted to convey a sense of its protagonist's unheralded confrontation with arbitrariness and irrationality, conditions qualifying all else that occurs in the novel. Joseph K.'s warders go on to eat his breakfast and confiscate his underwear, indications of the extremity and intrusiveness of the power the Court has usurped over his life. Already in this scene we find suggestive indications of the Court's obverse logic, the preconditions of an eventually emerging Discourse of the Law. In the scenario of its central character's progress through a domain of deranged but compelling logic, *The Trial* is not so remote from Lewis Carroll's *Alice in Wonderland* as it might seem to be. *The Trial* is Kafka's morose and ominous *Alice*. To establish the line, or rather departure, of this logic, I shall be splicing together a long extract from the pages immediately following the last substantial citation. This will be, along with the Parable of the Doorkeeper, my longest citation from the novel.

> "I'd better get Frau Grubach—" said K., as if wrenching himself away from the two men (though they were standing at quite a distance from him) and making as if to go out. "No," said the man at the window, flinging the book down on the table and getting up. "You can't go out, you are arrested." "So it seems," said K. "But what for?" he added. "We are not authorized to tell you that. Go to your room and wait there. Proceedings have been instituted against you, and you will be informed of everything in due course.

I am exceeding my instructions in speaking freely to you like this. But I hope nobody hears me except Franz, and he himself has been too free with you, against his express instructions. If you continue to have as good luck as you have had in the choice of your warders, then you can be confident of the final result." K. felt he must sit down, but now he saw that there was no seat in the whole room except the chair beside the window. "You'll soon discover that we're telling you the truth," said Franz. (*T*, 3)

Why didn't she [Frau Grubach] come in?" he asked. "She isn't allowed to," said the tall warder, "since you're under arrest." "But how can I be under arrest? And particularly in such a ridiculous fashion?" "So now you're beginning it all over again?" said the warder, dipping a slice of bread and butter into the honeypot. "We don't answer such questions." "You'll have to answer them," said K. "Here are my papers, now show me yours, and first of all your warrant for arresting me." "Oh good Lord," said the warder. "If you would only realize your position, and if you wouldn't insist on uselessly annoying us two, who probably mean better by you and stand closer to you than any other people in the world." . . . "Our officials, so far as I know them, and I know only the lowest grades among them, never go hunting for crime in the populace, but, as the Law decrees, are drawn toward the guilty and must then send out us warders. That is the Law. How could there be a mistake in that?" "I don't know this Law," said K. "All the worse for you," replied the warder. . . . "See, Willem, he admits that he doesn't know the Law and yet he claims he's innocent." "You're quite right, but you'll never make a man like that see reason," replied the other. K. gave no further answer; Must I, he thought, let myself be confused still worse by the gabble of those wretched hirelings?—they admit themselves that's all they are. . . . "And now I advise you," he went on, "to go to your room, stay quietly there, and wait for what may be decided about you. . . . You haven't treated us as our kind advances to you deserved, you have forgotten that we, no matter who we may be, are at least free men compared to you; that is no small advantage. All the same, we are prepared, if you have any money, to bring you a little breakfast from the coffeehouse across the street." (*T*, 5–7)

CODE

Logic. I cite these passages at length, because they are the first that register the paradoxical impact that the Law exerts upon its servants, victims, and readers. At the end of the first quotation, the warders assure Joseph K. that despite the incredible nature of present circumstances they are telling the truth. In miniature, this is the chief irony of the Law: outside its precincts, it appears, it is experienced as, arbitrary, irrational, cruel, inhuman. It would presume to separate Joseph K. from Frau Grubach, his residential manager of choice, a warder in civil terms, and the character closest to a mother who appears in the novel. But the Law, in terms of its internal sense and operations, like its servants in this scene, is telling the truth. The Law is, in other words, that which enunciates, and then violates, its own principles; that which exists on doubled, antithetical registers; that which is familiar and recognizable to K. (it eats the same breakfast and wears the same underwear), and yet which corresponds to and instruments alien and inhuman imperatives.

The universe of Immanuel Kant (1724–1804), a German philosopher with whom Kafka was familiar and who influenced other writers such as Kleist and Hoffmann whom Kafka read with great interest, is divided between human knowledge and experience and transcendental principles. The transcendental operates on the human world with the force of a moral imperative, but it can be known only tenuously, through a process of philosophical deduction. As Kant specifies in *The Critique of Pure Reason,* the relationship between the empirical and the transcendental worlds expresses itself only as a paradox.[4] Kant's scheme for the mutable and the immutable worlds, and any relation that takes place between them, is above all perspectival in nature. A glimpse of the transcendental "operating system" that governs human thought and knowledge does filter through to human understanding, but our knowledge of it invariably assumes the form of paradoxes, whose philosophical equivalents Kant calls antinomies. In the above-cited passages and throughout *The Trial,* K.'s experience of the Law is paradoxical or antinomian. It is possible to define Kafka's wider philosophical experiment in *The Trial* as a literary adaptation of the anomalies generated by the Kantian Law.

In the above passages, the Law insinuates itself into Joseph K.'s most familiar surroundings, yet it remains completely alien. It gives rise to fundamental questions, yet refuses to respond to inquiries. The workers inspire Joseph K. to produce all kinds of legal documents, yet are completely indifferent to them when they appear.

As chapter 1 develops, the fictive antinomies that Joseph K. encounters proliferate, setting a tone and establishing a logical model for the rest of the novel. Franz declares that the warders "probably mean better by you and stand closer to you than any other people in the world." On the same page he suggests that ignorance of the Law is more objectionable than the wrongdoings it proscribes. "What kind of man are you, then?" Joseph K. asks the Inspector. "You ask me to be sensible and you carry on in the most senseless way imaginable yourself. It's enough to sicken the dogs" (*T*, 13). (Note that a dog will be the excuse Joseph K. invents to camouflage the sounds of the whipping scene that takes place in the bank, and even more importantly, will exemplify, in his dying thought, the shame that constitutes the ongoing, nonimaginary punishment of *The Trial*.) The first chapter is a constricting network of antinomies, the most dramatic of which is that the trial will somehow render itself invisible, will disappear into the trappings of Joseph K.'s life, disturbing, at most, a few photos on the wall of Fräulein Bürstner's room. "You are under arrest certainly, but that need not hinder you from going about your business. Nor will you be prevented from leading your ordinary life," declares the Inspector (*T*, 14).

Are these conditions the mark of madness, of some completely disorganized set of delusions? Not if we give some attention to the specificities of the text. "Our officials," pronounce the warders in the above passage, "never go hunting for crime in the populace, but, as the Law decrees, are drawn toward the guilty." Joseph K. may well experience his arrest as a shot in the dark, or at least out of the blue, but as a Kafkan son, in the context of the readings we explored in chapter 4, he bears a legacy of familiar guilt and artistic intuition. Like the most unforgettable protagonists in world literature, such as Oedipus and

Hamlet (and like the exemplary first subjects of psychoanalysis whose case histories were recorded by Freud),[5] Joseph K. is guilty of violating the Law long before he becomes conscious of the crime he has committed. His knowledge is realistic, even lucid, but hopelessly belated. Joseph K.'s crime is not an act or even any evil intention; it is this belatedness of understanding, this unconsciousness, that he happens to share, by structural necessity, with every other human being. "No one but you could gain admittance through this door," specifies the doorkeeper of the pivotal Parable. But the knowledge that would have prompted this entry and this escape arrives by necessity, by Law, inevitably too late.

The paradoxes of the Law belong not to its violations but to its very nature. The warders and their messages can only appear, to Joseph K. and the novel's readers alike, as ridiculous and absurd. Yet there is another sense, the transcendental's understanding of itself, in which everything the warders say is realistic and true. It is the nature of the artwork to sustain and arise from this tension. For this reason, the most striking illuminations of the Law in the novel assume the form of anecdotes, parables, and portraits. The artwork is the medium, for Kafka as well as for Kant, through which the inscrutable workings of the transcendental upon the human environment make themselves intelligible.

For this reason, in spite of Joseph K.'s sense of superiority, the warders of this scene and other Court officials in the novel are, for all their obtuseness and venality, as important to its process as Joseph K. is. While Joseph K., exercising a perfectly understandable common sense carried over from the empirical world, attempts to destroy the Law's paradoxes by penetrating through to their truth or falsity, the servants of the Court calmly reassert the anomalies and vacancies inherent to the human intellectual condition. As Joseph K. absorbs the Law's paradoxical conditions, he gains the sensibility of the artist as defined by the Western tradition of aesthetics, just in time, unfortunately, for his execution. By a certain perverse logic at the very heart of aesthetic production and literary inventiveness, Joseph K. has indeed been fortunate in the particular choice of his warders, and calm deliberation will be the most productive attitude in addressing the Law's inconceivable conditions.

The Trial is on many readers' "short lists" of works exemplifying literary thought and creativity in part because it is so densely written, because few of its seemingly random details do not eventually find some broader significance within the cohesive-repetitive fabric of the novel. I have dwelt so long on the first few pages to anticipate the value and importance even of some of the absurdest circumstances. My commentary has assumed the deliberate form of a semiological analysis in order to "flag" certain images, modes, and devices from the beginning of the text, so that readers will be free to pursue these "files," if they are of any suggestive value to them. The remainder of chapter 1 and Joseph K.'s behavior before the Examining Magistrate in chapter 2 are of great moment to the overall development of *The Trial* and its literary, philosophical, and theoretical ideas. I will continue the very deliberate manner of my semiological analysis until we have arrived at a preliminary reading of the passages in question. When the purpose of such a procedure is complete, my commentary will assume the more conventional form of a running literary interpretation.

> She was sitting darning at a table, on which lay a heap of old stockings. . . . He gazed at Frau Grubach with a certain gratitude. "Why are you still working at this late hour?" he asked. . . . "I'm afraid I've been responsible for giving you extra work today." "How is that?" she asked, becoming more intent, the work resting in her lap. "I mean the men who were here this morning." . . . "No, that can't happen again," she said reassuringly, with an almost sorrowful smile. "Do you really mean it?" asked K. "Yes," she said softly, "and above all you mustn't take it too much to heart. Lots of things happen in this world! As you've spoken so frankly to me, Herr K., I may as well admit to you that I listened for a little behind the door and that the two warders told me a few things too. It's a matter of your happiness, and I really have that at heart, more perhaps than I should, for I am only your landlady. Well, then, I heard a few things, but I can't say that they were particularly bad. No. You are under arrest, certainly, but not

as a thief is under arrest. If one's arrested as a thief, that's a bad business, but as for this arrest—. It gives me the feeling of something very learned, forgive me if what I say is stupid, it gives me the feeling of something learned which I don't understand, but which there is no need to understand." (*T*, 18–19)

AMBIANCE

Ordinariness. The scene in which Joseph K. and Frau Grubach sit together the evening of the arrest while the latter darns stockings stands out in the novel for its peaceful domesticity. The unsettling irony upon which the narrative plays here is that Frau Grubach, even while professing her ignorance, is more learned in the ways of the Law than her successful tenant. The sorrowful smile with which she acknowledges that today's arrest was a one-time occurrence betrays a wisdom in these matters of which Joseph K. remains ignorant.

What is the nature of the Law that it could be familiar to the most ordinary landlady (and the audience of other normal citizens she epitomizes) and inscrutable to the successful chief clerk at a bank and son of a family? The answer that the text furnishes to this question in this section of the narrative has much to do with ordinariness. Legal matters may give Frau Grubach "the feeling of something very learned" but when she greets Joseph K. she "was most cordial and would hear of no apology." The Law that has arrested K. is to some extent the Law of the Ordinary, a code of tolerance toward, patience for, and ultimately, acquiescence to the limits and emotional restraints of polite society. Joseph K., a sensitive, questioning character, is as alien to this aspect of the Law as Frau Grubach and the elderly spectator of earlier scenes may find the complications of atomic physics.

The Law of the Ordinary is the sociological extension of the physical law of gravity that so thwarted the obsessive wishes of the trapeze artist in "First Sorrow." In *The Trial*, the son of a family with artistic sensibilities responds to the restraints of the Ordinary with a mixture of impatience, frustration, and contempt. Kafka was not the only major literary figure of his era to measure the impact of the social pressure to conform to certain ideals irreproachable in themselves upon the artistic performance. James Joyce named Stephen Dedalus, the hero of *Portrait of the Artist as a Young Man* and *Ulysses,* after Daedalus, the mythical Greek artificer who discerned the secret of flight but who lost his son Icarus to the latter's inability to heed his warning: Don't fly too high, don't fly too close to the sun. In Joyce's novels, the social restrictions upon artistic pretensions assume more concrete and realistic forms than they do in Kafka's: they issue from church and state and exert a repressive impact upon family. Stephen Dedalus's most defiant act in *Ulysses* is to refuse to participate in the religious ceremonies surrounding his mother's death. This provocation costs him dearly on an "emotional" level, but his *non serviam*—"I shall not serve"—directed toward organized religion and state ideology remains firm. In Kafka, the forms of emotional blackmail that encroach upon the artist-son for his singularity are more subtle and issue from a more diffuse set of sources. But the protagonist feels their threat to his work and self every bit as intensely.

Joseph K. responds to the restraining pressure of the Ordinary with a number of defenses, including contempt. "You're too unyielding, that's what I've heard," Leni will tell him (*T,* 108). Of this flaw, hubris, pride, the classical defect of tragedy, Joseph K. is indeed guilty, perhaps even before the novel begins. As the narrative specifies, he responds to the three fellow bank employees who accompany the Inspector at his arrest as "insignificant anemic young men" (*T,* 15). There is something tragic about this sense of superiority, justifying the inclusion of martyrdom in Kafka's updated trinity, because its critical detachment does belong to the aesthetic enterprise. There will be more on Joseph K.'s alternation between contempt and shame below, with respect to his appearance before the Examining Magistrate.

> "Look here," she cried, "my photographs are all mixed up! That is really odious. So someone has actually been in my room who had no right to come in." K. nodded and silently cursed the clerk Kaminer, who could never control his stupid, meaningless fidget-

ing. "It is curious," said Fräulein Bürstner, "that I should be compelled now to forbid you to do something which you ought to forbid yourself to do, that is to enter my room in my absence." "But I have explained to you, Fräulein," said K., going over to the photographs, "that it was not I who interfered with these photographs. . . . There was a Court of Inquiry here today." "On your account?" asked the Fräulein. "Yes," said K. "Why, do you think I must be innocent?" "Well, innocent," said Fräulein Bürstner, . . . "I don't really know you; all the same, it must be a serious crime that would bring a Court of Inquiry down on a man." . . . "You see," said K., "you haven't much experience in legal matters." "No, I haven't," said Fräulein Bürstner, "and I have often regretted it, for I would like to know everything there is to know, and law courts interest me particularly. A court of law has a curious attraction, hasn't it? But I'll soon remedy my ignorance in that respect, for next month I am joining the clerical staff of a lawyer's office." (*T*, 24–25)

CODES

Law and sexuality, the juncture of the two quintessential forms of guilt. The Court, with its uncanny powers of withdrawal and self-erasure, has left only one trace of the earlier proceedings in Frau Grubach's apartment, a slight disorder in Fräulein Bürstner's photographs, dream images of a normal working girl. Experience, the passage would establish, is all on the side of the males. Guilt, like the constraint of art (think here of hunger artistry), is a male property and burden. Its chief payoff, an ambivalent one in Kafka, is the attraction it exerts on women. "I seem to recruit women helpers, he thought almost in surprise; first Fräulein Bürstner, then the wife of the usher, and now this little nurse who appears to have some incomprehensible desire for me," reports the narrative of K.'s thoughts when he is with Leni (*T*, 109). In the scene cited immediately above, Fräulein Bürstner has just returned from the theater; she is on her way to becoming an employee of the Law.

"May I shift this night table from beside your bed?" "What an idea!" cried Fräulein Bürstner. "Of course not!" "Then I can't show you how it happened," said K. in agitation. . . . . "Oh, if you need it for your performance, shift the table by all means," said Fräulein Bürstner. . . . K. stationed the table in the middle of the room and sat down behind it. "You must picture to yourself exactly where the various people are, it's very interesting. I am the Inspector, over there on the chest two warders are sitting, beside the photographs three young men are standing. . . . I'm standing here in front of the table. The Inspector is lounging at his ease with his legs crossed, his arm hanging over the back of the chair like this, an absolute boor. And now we can really begin. The Inspector shouts as if he had to waken me out of my sleep, he actually bawls; I'm afraid, if I am to make you understand, I'll have to bawl too, but he only bawls my name." Fräulein Bürstner, who was listening with amusement, put her finger to her lips to keep K. from shouting, but it was too late, K. was too absorbed in his role, he gave a long-drawn shout: "Joseph K." (*T,* 26–27)

GENRE

Theater, or rather mixed media. The first of the novel's three scenes of relaxed sexuality, in which Joseph K. interacts with his most viable partner, passes in a dramatic re-creation of the arrest, the preliminary declaration of guilt. The internal conflict of guilt is dramatic in nature. Theater is the "natural" medium for the acting out or dramatization of this conflict. Its creation becomes the occasion for a musical accompaniment for seduction, to which Fräulein Bürstner is evidently susceptible.

The medium of theater enables Joseph K. to be, at least momentarily and "for pretend," his persecutor, the Inspector, and to gain mastery over the situation in at least this sense. (The fact that as a boy Franz Kafka organized his siblings to present family theatricals may be of interest here.) If the fiction of theater enables Joseph K., who first forgets to include himself in the scene and then occupies the most important place, to gain a temporary control over his circumstances, what would be the analogous role of fiction writing in the life of Franz Kafka?

"Doing" theater, dramatizing "internal" conflicts and desires, is, in this scene, a sexual activity. Theatricality is quintessentially sexual in nature. Sexuality consists of far more than the sexual impulse, the Freudian drive. It fulfills itself in acts, ones that in Kafka require a collaboration between actors and an audience.

> But now go, leave me to myself, I need more than ever to be left in peace. . . . K. clasped her hand and then her wrist. "But you aren't angry with me?" he asked. She shook his hand off and answered: "No, no, I'm never angry with anybody." He felt for her wrist again, she let him take it this time and so led him to the door. . . . "Now, please do come! Look"—she pointed to the Captain's door, underneath which showed a strip of light—"he has turned on his light and is amusing himself at our expense." "I'm just coming," K. said, rushed out, seized her, and kissed her first on the lips, then all over the face, like some thirsty animal lapping greedily at a spring of long-sought fresh water. Finally he kissed her on the neck, right on the throat, and kept his lips there for a long time. A slight noise from the Captain's room made him look up. "I'm going now," he said; he wanted to call Fräulein Bürstner by her first name, but he did not know what it was. (*T*, 29)

SCENARIO

For the benefit of the Captain. Artistry and desire comprise the son's primal guilts, his doubled mark of Cain. Artistry and desire oppose and surpass the father and paternal authority; they are performed, incidentally, for the father's benefit. I note here that K.'s other flirtations in the novel are with women "already accounted for." His sexuality is one of fleeting, short-lived infatuations. The Court usher's wife in chapters 2 and 3 answers to three men at once: the Examining Magistrate, student Bertold, and last and least, her husband; Leni ministers to Joseph K.'s attorney. K.'s infatuations not only constitute a message to the men involved: in light of his legal problems and needs, his choices of women (and their attraction to him) are disastrous. As impulsive as Joseph K. is in the above scene (and surprise attack is one of the oppressed son's few weapons, against women *and* fathers), he is ignorant of Fräulein Bürstner's first name, she is not quite real to him—just as he initially overlooked himself in his dramatic re-creation of his arrest. K.'s most sustained and self-directed expression of desire in the novel, his best seduction performance, receives its illumination from the long finger of light issuing from the Captain's room.

My very deliberate attention to details evident in the first chapter of *The Trial* takes place in the hope that the images and devices I am "flagging" at the very beginning will be of service as readers decode and interpret the novel for themselves. In closing the present chapter, I wish to devote the same type of attention to one or two passages describing another of Joseph K.'s performances, before the Examining Magistrate, even though they are located in chapter 2 of the novel.

> K. was informed by telephone that next Sunday a short inquiry into his case would take place. His attention was drawn to the fact that these inquiries would now follow each other regularly, perhaps not every week, but at more frequent intervals as time went on. It was in the general interest, on the one hand, that the case should be quickly concluded, but on the other hand the interrogations must be thorough in every respect, although because of the strain involved, they must never last too long. (*T*, 31)

TONE

Ominousness, inevitability.

STYLE

Passive constructions such as "was informed by telephone" combine with conditional tenses and a subjunctive tentativeness ("would take place," "would now follow") to convey a double impression of uncertainty from K.'s point of view and of omniscient secrecy and control emanating from the powers that be. The Court specifies and enacts the imperatives of the situation: "the case should be quickly concluded, but . . . the interrogations must be thorough in every respect."

PLOT

At the beginning of chapter 2, however, K. has not one but two conversations around the telephone. The first may emphasize a certain disarray and powerlessness that have crept into his life, but the second underlines a tangible success that he has begun to achieve.

> "Bad news?" asked the Assistant Manager casually, not really wanting to know but merely eager to get K. away from the telephone. "No, no," said K., stepping aside but without going away. The Assistant Manager lifted the receiver and said, speaking round it while he waited to be connected: "Oh, a word with you, Herr K. Would you do me the favor of joining a party on my yacht on Sunday morning? . . . K. made an effort to attend to what the Assistant Manager was saying. . . . The Assistant Manager had definitely humbled himself in giving this invitation, even though he had merely dropped it casually while waiting at the telephone to get a connection. Yet K. had to humble the man a second time, for he said: "Thanks very much. But I'm sorry I have no time on Sunday, I have a previous engagement." "A pity," said the Assistant Manager, turning to speak into the telephone. (*T*, 32–33)

CODES

Art, torment, life. The Assistant Manager's generous act, indicative both of his good will and of K.'s centrality to the bank, coincides temporally with K.'s inability to enjoy it and benefit from it. The trial, whether we think of it as psychological torment, artistic intuition, or social alienation or persecution, has become a parasitic secret (or not so secret) second life, sapping the energies and nullifying the achievements of K.'s "first" or apparent life. (It is in this sense that the trial plays an analogous role to Gregor Samsa's insect carapace in "The Metamorphosis.") As the novel proceeds, Joseph K. pays increasing attention to the internal drama of his trial, and is correspondingly less capable of responding to his existential tasks, projects, and accomplishments. The trial becomes a kind of static interference blurring the communication between Joseph K. and his world. (It is for this reason, perhaps, that the telephone is an important appliance in this scene.) There is a symbiotic, mutually dependent relationship between the trial and Joseph K.'s life: the torment, persecution, or artistic intuition of the trial become more prominent the more active and successful K.'s interests become. The more K. achieves, the more he is primed to suffer.

AFFECTS

Shame and pity. The Assistant Manager, in order to invite K. to his yachting party, has had to swallow his pride. The emotional background for K.'s outrageous and unexpected performance at his "first interrogation" is a capacity for superiority and even contempt masked beneath a pervasive sense of inadequacy and shame. The interrogation surely befuddles us because it places on display, seemingly without precedent, K.'s assertion of his superiority and importance. The initial passages of chapter 2 offer us, however, if we attend to them, ample clues as to K.'s intense concern with his status in relation to those around him and with competitively maintaining his advantages.

On his way to the first interrogation, for example, K. catches sight of Rabensteiner, Kullich, and Kaminer, the "subordinate employees of the Bank" whom the narrator, betraying K.'s thoughts, had described as "insignificant anemic young men" when they had participated in his arrest. In the second chapter,

> All three were probably staring after him and wondering where
> their chief was rushing off to; a sort of defiance had kept K. from
> taking a vehicle to his destination, he loathed the thought of char-
> tering anyone, even the most casual stranger, to help him along in
> this case of his, also he did not want to be beholden to anyone or
> to initiate anyone even remotely in his affairs, and last of all he
> had no desire to belittle himself before the Court of Inquiry by a
> too scrupulous punctuality. Nevertheless he was hurrying so as to
> arrive by nine o'clock if possible, although he had not even been
> required to appear at any specified time. (T, 33–34)

The glimpse of these inferiors accompanies an account of K.'s painful
awareness of his status and appearance in any situation and of his
extreme reluctance to solicit or receive help, as if these acts would
amount to a constitutional crisis in his competence. K.'s concern with
the appearance of his autonomy and control over circumstances here is
so great that he in fact allows himself very little room in which to
operate. "A too scrupulous punctuality" is as odious to him as delaying
a driver or arriving unconscionably late, the latter of which he eventually does. K. becomes a parody of assertiveness and self-control when
he addresses the Court of Inquiry, but his traumatized mastery is rooted in an overall atmosphere of defensive thought and maneuvers.

> But Juliusstrasse, where the house was said to be and at whose
> end he stopped for a moment, displayed on both sides houses
> almost exactly alike, high gray tenements inhabited by poor peo-
> ple. This being Sunday morning, most of the windows were occu-
> pied, men in shirt-sleeves were leaning there smoking or holding
> small children cautiously and tenderly on the window ledges.
> Other windows were piled high with bedding, above which the
> disheveled head of a woman would appear for a moment. People
> were shouting to one another across the street; one shout just
> above K.'s head caused great laughter. Down the whole length of
> the street at regular intervals, below the level of the pavement,
> there were little general grocery shops, to which short flights of
> steps led down. Women were thronging into and out of these
> shops or gossiping on the steps outside. (T, 34)

SETTING

Social.

CODE

Social class. The narrative does not content itself with K.'s pained awareness of his personal status; it encompasses the wider social dimension and implications of K.'s trial. The awareness of poor factory working conditions and the hazards of mechanized labor that Kafka had gained from his experience as a member of the legal staff of insurance companies handling workman's compensation cases made him, according to Klaus Wagenbach, "the only 'bourgeois' writer of his time who had such first-hand knowledge" of industrial exploitation and its consequences" (Wagenbach, 104).

AMBIANCE

Ordinariness, simplicity. Kafka approaches Dostoyevski and Camus here in the vividness with which he depicts the ordinary, unadorned life. For all his achievements and importance, Joseph K. is prevented from joining this scene. In this wide-angle still life of ordinary humanity, the men in shirt sleeves and disheveled women are interpenetrated by the Law. It lives literally on top of them. But K. is the individual for whom an unrelenting torment has begun.

> At the doors which were shut K. knocked and asked if a joiner called Lanz lived there. Generally a woman opened, listened to his questions, and then turned to someone in the room, who thereupon rose from the bed. "The gentleman's asking if a joiner called Lanz lives here." "A joiner called Lanz?" asked the man from the bed. "Yes," said K., though it was beyond question that the Court of Inquiry did not sit here and his inquiry

was therefore superfluous. Many seemed convinced that it was highly important for K. to find the joiner Lanz, they took a long time to think it over, suggested some joiner who, however, was not called Lanz, or a name which had some quite distant resemblance to Lanz, or inquired of their neighbors, or escorted K. to a door some considerable distance away, where they fancied such a man might be living as a lodger, or where there was someone who could give better information than they could. . . . But then the uselessness of the whole expedition filled him with exasperation, he went up the stairs once more and knocked at the first door he came to on the fifth story. The first thing he saw in the little room was a great pendulum clock which already pointed to ten. "Does a joiner called Lanz live here?" he asked. "Please go through," said a young woman with sparkling black eyes, who was washing children's clothes in a tub, and she pointed with her damp hand to the open door of the next room.

K. felt as though he were entering a meeting-hall. (*T*, 36–37)

MODE

Allegory. The overview of suffering-thriving-persisting humanity continues when the setting shifts to the indoors of the tenements also inhabited by the Court. In order to locate the chamber to which he has been summoned without divulging his situation (and without incurring any debt of gratitude), Joseph K. invents a story and a character, joiner Lanz. In this act, he steps into the role and function of the novelist. The confused reaction of the residents to his story demonstrates that it has complicated matters as much as it has been useful. The narrative leaves open the possibility that the ordinary-seeming residents know more about K.'s situation and better interest than he does, in which case his dissimulation works to a negative effect. K. bases his invention in part on the name of Captain Lanz, Frau Grubach's nephew, who has moved into her apartment.

MODE

Humor.

CODE

Theology, Jewish. For K. to claim that he is searching for joiner Lanz is something of a joke, a Jewish joke at that. The name *Lanz* is homonymic to (sounds like) *Lands,* in German the possessive form of the noun designating land or the country. In the consummate Parable of the Doorkeeper in chapter 9, the individual who waits a lifetime at the entrance to the Law only to learn its inscrutable paradox is described as "a man from the country" *(ein Mann vom Lande).* The rural nature of this exemplary reader's origins is in keeping with the parable's fundamental, near-universal message. To be a man from the country is also to be a *Landsmann,* a countryman, a child of one's native land, akin to the Italian *paisano,* whose Yiddish form in the plural is *Landesleut.* In inventing joiner Lanz, K. thinks he is throwing his interlocutors off track when in fact he is revealing his urgent quest for his counterparts, his *semblables,* ultimately, for himself. The decoy or simulacrum he is seeking is simpler, more fundamental, than himself, not the chief clerk of a bank but a joiner, not an opener of riddles but an assembler of answers.

CODE

Social class. The alter ego that K. invents for himself is a tradesman rather than an executive. His honest response to the Examining Magistrate's query as to his profession ("you are a house painter?" [*T,* 40]) is greeted with a "hearty outburst of laughter" from the right-hand side of the divided chamber audience. The alter ego, the alternate version of himself that Joseph K. contends and is confused with, is of a lower social status and class than the ambitious, overachieving bank executive. Like Jacob wrestling with the angel in Genesis, Joseph K. grapples with the tradesman in himself.

SETTING

Space. K. passes directly from a private room, in which a woman does her wash, into a hearing chamber owned by the Court. A laundry room transforms itself into an official setting; "a woman with sparkling black eyes" metamorphoses herself into the Court usher's wife (and, eventually, the Examining Magistrate's mistress). The Court penetrates into the innermost recesses of one's private life, yet is alien, inscrutable, in its procedures. The uncanny defamiliarization effected by the Court takes place immediately, with the directedness of Freudian condensation and poetic metonymy, with the suddenness of the Freudian joke. Such sudden transformations set the tone for Joseph K.'s subsequent wanderings through living and working spaces—even an artist's atelier and a cathedral—eventually revealed as belonging to the Court (see *T*, 150).

> He had involuntarily raised his voice. Someone in the audience clapped his hands high in the air and shouted: "Bravo! Why not? Bravo! And bravo again!" . . . "I have no wish to shine as an orator," said K., having come to this conclusion, "nor could I if I wished. The Examining Magistrate, no doubt, is much the better speaker, it is part of his vocation. All I desire is the public ventilation of a public grievance. Listen to me. Some ten days ago I was arrested, in a manner that seems ridiculous even to myself, though that is immaterial at the moment. . . . These warders, moreover, were degenerate ruffians, they deafened my ears with their gabble, they tried to induce me to bribe them, they attempted to get my clothes and underclothes from me under dishonest pretexts, they asked me to give them money ostensibly to bring me some breakfast after they had brazenly eaten my own breakfast under my eyes. . . . But that is not all, he [the Inspector] had brought three minor employees of my Bank into the lady's [Fräulein Bürstner's] room, who amused themselves by fingering and disarraying cer-

tain photographs, the property of the lady. The presence of these employees had another object as well, of course, they were expected, like my landlady and her maid, to spread the news of my arrest, damage my public reputation, and in particular shake my position in the Bank." (*T*, 42–44)

CODE

Theology. The buzzing room, strewn with books, with its unintelligible controversies and the beards and unidentifiable badges worn by its audience, is highly suggestive of a Talmudic academy. This is a setting likely to be imagined with a mixture of sentimental pride and bemused wonderment by someone of Franz Kafka's family, class, and attainments.

AFFECT

Contempt and shame. The overarching irony of Joseph K.'s interrogation before the Examining Magistrate—the equivalent of a logical antinomy in fiction—is that our protagonist, in heroically gathering his forces and asserting himself, from a point of view that he inevitably experiences, is actually ruining his chance for mounting a successful defense, assuming any such chances exist for him. Joseph K.'s audience at the interrogation, at least a healthy segment of it, treats his self-assertion with unabashed mockery. It is easy to overlook, in light of the hard-won insistence and severity of K.'s assertions, their grounding in his extreme lack of confidence and in his faulty attentiveness to himself. The more K. agitates himself in order to express his grievances, the more he reveals his personal insecurity. K. pushes himself to greater heights of insistence and even arrogance in his performance before the Court of Inquiry, but the foundation of his contemptuous attitude is a pervasive sense of shame. Shame is the prevalent emotion by which K. expresses his shaken confidence in himself.

At the beginning of the lengthy quotation just cited, K. is in a state of disbelief that his words and gestures provoke any reactions whatsoever on the part of his auditors. His account of his legal misfortunes thus far already constitutes his second dramatic and narrative re-creation of these events (the first was for Fräulein Bürstner's benefit). Joseph K.'s account this time around emphasizes the Court employees' disregard for his socioeconomic status, the possibility that the affair will make him lose face in the eyes of "a lady whom I deeply respect," and its "damage" to his "public reputation." This constitutes a highly defensive reaction to the situation at best. Here the narrative suggests that Joseph K.'s personal fragility brings his trial upon him. His pervasive insecurity is the trial before the trial. Such a character attracts social disapproval just as he prompts recognition by other guilty souls and the connivance of mothering females.

> "There can be no doubt—" said K., quite softly . . . "there can be no doubt that behind all the actions of this court of justice, that is to say in my case, behind my arrest and today's interrogation, there is a great organization at work. An organization which not only employs corrupt warders, oafish Inspectors, and Examining Magistrates of whom the best that can be said is that they recognize their own limitations, but also has at its disposal a judicial hierarchy of high, indeed of the highest rank, with an indispensable and numerous retinue of servants, clerks, police, and other assistants, perhaps even hangmen, I do not shrink from that word. And the significance of this great organization, gentlemen? It consists in this, that innocent persons are accused of guilt, and senseless proceedings are put in motion against them, mostly without effect, it is true, as in my own case. But considering the senselessness of the whole, how is it possible for the higher ranks to prevent gross corruption in their agents? It is impossible. Even the highest Judge in this organization cannot resist it. So the warders try to steal the clothes off the bodies of the people they arrest, the Inspectors break into strange houses, and innocent men, instead of being fairly examined, are humiliated in the presence of public assemblies." (T, 45–46)

MODE

Discourse of the Accused. In response to the coldly indifferent and antinomian Discourse of the Law arises the (legally and personally) defensive Discourse of the Accused, itself a recognizable descendent of the Discourse of the Son. Let us recall, in relation to "The Judgment," how arbitrary and cruel the father's accusations sounded; how self-righteously, almost smugly, the son couched his efforts on behalf of his outmoded father and defeated friend. In the passage just quoted K.'s eloquence, fueled by an ample supply of contempt, rises to the pitch of messianic social criticism and to the drama of all-pervasive corruption and conspiracy. Yet if our criteria for truth in this case are based on the "data" that the narrative has provided, every pronouncement that K. makes is true; every inference he draws is likely! This is the basic paradox or antinomy implicit to the Discourse of the Accused (Son): it is powered by a collaboration of shame and contempt, yet within its confines it is true; just as the Discourse of the Law (Father) is accusatory, unsympathetic, and self-contradictory. The Discourse of the Accused is at once self-righteous and thoroughly admirable, demonstrating a genuine repugnance at injustice and concern for the downtrodden. In response to the indifferent and authoritarian but idealistic Discourse of the Law arises the contemptuous Discourse of the Accused, itself paradoxical. The dénouement, or resolution, of *The Trial* may to some extent be regarded as the interplay and working through of these antithetical truths.

Joseph K.'s bizarre and arbitrary trial is thus lost before it is won. It is housed in a setting, ornamented by images and couched in a style and vocabularies (rhetorics) whose justification and operating principles I have begun to sketch out in detail. The specifics to which I have pointed proliferate themselves and intertwine as *The Trial* builds to its hopeless, untenable, and fundamentally human impasse and culmination.

6

Bearings

As I suggested above, *The Trial,* like all important works of literature regardless of genre, is a densely written text. That is, there is an intertwining of its resonant images and figures of speech, an expansion of significance effected by this process of recombination, and a parallelism between this literary enrichment and the reader's interpretative capabilities to discern and unravel the meaning of his or her experience. We have already covered considerable territory in identifying the ongoing themes and devices constitutive of *The Trial*'s drama and significance. In what consists its further dramatic, ideational, and artistic development?

I would like to approach this question, before moving on to the novel's middle chapters and tragic-intellectual climax, in three ways: in terms of plot, inter "personal" dynamics, and artistic understanding. With regard to K.'s "existence," the trial plays an increasingly weighty, distracting, and energy-sapping role, eventually taking on the same "importance" as his life, in effect becoming tantamount to it, becoming a "complementary" existence, usurping its place. We have already begun to see that the trial, in many respects, corresponds to certain fundamental features of human psychological and interpersonal life. *The Trial*'s plot records the trial's progressive impact upon Joseph K.'s work at the bank, interactions with his family (as represented by Uncle Karl and his daughter, Erna), and friendly and sexual relationships. Interpersonally, K. undergoes a gradual social isolation as the novel develops, whose culminating act is the dismissal of Lawyer Huld, who, despite his infirmity, is the last character in the novel to articulate and advance K.'s interest. (K.'s increasing social alienation in the novel is reminiscent of the diminishing contact with human society and physical isolation that Captain Ahab and the members of the *Pequod*'s crew experience in *Moby-Dick*.) Yet for all these untoward, emotionally troubling developments in Joseph K.'s "life," the novel also records an increasing understanding (that the protagonist shares with the reader) of the artwork as the process and location in which the conflicts, loneliness, frustrations, and tragedy of human life can be worked through, understood, and metamorphosed into something of empathy and beauty. In particular, the literary artwork, as elaborated in the Parable of the Doorkeeper and rehearsed prior to it in the novel, transforms the bewilderment of conflict into the combinatory insight of interpretation. The literary artwork represents, dramatizes, and *becomes* the interpretative process through which the tragedy of life acquires, if nothing else, certain possibilities of meaning.

In chapters 2–5 of the novel, the initial conditions of Joseph K.'s psychological, social, and physical lives consolidate themselves. Not until the homoerotic, sadomasochistically tinged whipping scene of chapter 5 do the full implications of K.'s arrest and its bizarre intellectual premises register themselves. We can think of chapters 5–8 as concerning the trial's tightening grip on Joseph K., at the same time that his hold on his professional tasks and duties, his relationships, and even his sensible promotion of his own self-interest falters. As this latter process takes place, however, the Law reveals itself to be possessed of an intricacy and complexity that are ultimately artistic in their nature and beautiful in their effect. This increasing aesthetic sense and interpretative awareness may comprise the Son of Guilt's only, but substantial, reward, his bittersweet patrimony. Chapters 7 and 8 are notable because in them the trial's conceptual and aesthetic properties begin to assume the same importance as the distraction, inconvenience, shame, and physical exhaustion it causes. On a superficial level, Tradesman Block's account of his experience as a perpetual defendant and Court artist Titorelli's discussion of the logically complementary, unattainable forms of acquittal "available" to K. only seem to further the perversity of the Court's logic and the inevitability of its destruction. But K. is also privy to the irony, humor, and ingeniousness of these narrations. Prepared for the blinding insight of the Parable of the Doorkeeper by these absurd revelations about the Law and its language, K. meets his death far more as an artist, or at least as a critic of aesthetic and intellectual processes, than he was at the moment of his arrest. In this sense, the end of his life has been the edification of his interpretative powers.

The processes of loss, learning, revelation, and tragic death that I described in the preceding paragraph have deep roots in the history of literature. Kafka was able to "tap into" the tragic, epic, scriptural, and parodic roots of literature at the same time that he was frustrating the standard literary expectations of his readers, and, through a process of disfiguration, producing hybrid works of striking novelty. Kafka could invade the history of literature at the same time that he was knocking the stuffing out of it. In this respect, like other major modernists such as James Joyce, Marcel Proust, Gertrude Stein, Ezra Pound, and T. S. Eliot, Kafka was a comparatist before there was a comparative literature discipline.

With respect to chapters 2–5, I will devote attention to the emerging Court's environmental qualities, such as space, light, and air, and to the trial's impact upon the sexual dimension of Joseph K.'s "life." (Sexuality, in literature, has never been merely one arena of human experience among others. It has often acquired an exemplary status, "stood for"—as a synecdoche—the entire range of intellectual, emotive, and artistic sensibilities and developmental potentials.) In my analysis of chapters 5–8, I will focus on the Court's emerging interpretative and aesthetic qualities, and upon K.'s concurrent withdrawal from his everyday associations and concerns.

THE ENVIRONMENT OF THE CONTRARY

In short, the Court spaces intrude where others end; enclose where others would open up; withdraw where others would remain in permanence. The air within its installations is so thin from overuse (an environmental analogue to endless interpretation) that it cannot sustain new arrivals from the outside world. Like the obverse side of Lewis Carroll's looking-glass, the Court environment, an interpretative-literary domain, is the contrary of everything it would take to support everyday life or promote common sense.

The Court space—like God in Judeo-Christian theology—is both everywhere and nowhere. It erases all, or almost all, traces of its presence during Joseph K.'s arrest in Frau Grubach's apartment. It invades the living quarters of tenements set amid the dreariness common to certain European suburbs. We have already seen Joseph K. stumble upon his hearing directly from a laundry room in the tenement. Joseph K.'s progression as he gets his bearings in the domains of the Court and the Law is tantamount to learning the singular qualities of their space, to breathing in their overburdened atmosphere.

The Court is a space in which the Examining Magistrate can suddenly appear at the foot of the Court usher's bed in the middle of the night, in order to admire his wife's beauty (*T*, 54–55), and in which the same woman can be literally snatched from K.'s arms by the lean and hungry student and delivered to the same Examining Magistrate, her husband's employer (*T*, 59). Domestic space, the Court usher's parlor, doubles as an official installation, the vestibule to the Examining Chamber. In the domain of the Law, corrupt officials, whose legal tracts turn out to be works of smut (*How Grete Was Plagued by Her Husband Hans* [*T*, 52]) live in close contact with the servants they dominate and exploit, and with the students who double as their henchmen. This architectural arrangement is held together by nothing more imposing than a rickety set of stairs.

> The little wooden stairway did not reveal anything, no matter how long one regarded it. But K. noticed a small card pinned up

beside it, and crossing over he read in childish, unpracticed hand-writing: "Law Court Offices upstairs." So the Law Court offices were up in the attics of this tenement? That was not an arrange-ment likely to inspire much respect, and for an accused man it was reassuring to reckon how little money this Court could have at its disposal when it housed its offices in a part of the building where the tenants, who themselves belonged to the poorest of the poor, flung their useless lumber. (*T*, 59–60)

Through such an inadequate structure, identified with childlike impre-cision, are communicated the determinations and specifications, even the carnal desires, of the Law.

"And he writes out so many reports. You say that the officials are lazy, but that certainly doesn't apply to all of them, particularly to the Examining Magistrate, he's always writing," reports the Court usher's wife, who, according to her bemused husband, has flung her-self at the powerful official as often as he has sought her out (*T*, 54). The Court is a domain of hyperacting and hyperwriting, the interpre-tative process intensified to the *n*th degree. It is the hub in a commu-nications network whose messages are, at one and the same time, administrative, theoretical, sexual, and aesthetic in nature. The Court atmosphere collapses these very different messages to the same status and treats them in the same way. As in so many areas of twentieth-century life, the facilities lag far behind the concepts and the freedom they facilitate.

On entering he almost stumbled, for behind the door there was an extra step. "They don't show much consideration for the public," he said. "They show no consideration of any kind," replied the usher. "Just look at this waitingroom." It was a long passage, a lobby communicating by ill-fitting doors with the different offices on the floor. Although there was no window to admit light, it was not entirely dark, for some of the offices were not properly board-ed off from the passage but had an open frontage of wooden rails, reaching, however, to the roof, through which a little light pene-trated and through which one could see a few officials as well, some writing at their desks, and some standing close to the rails peering through the interstices at the people in the lobby. There were only a few people in the lobby, probably because it was Sunday. They made a very modest showing. At almost regular intervals they were sitting singly along a row of wooden benches fixed to either side of the passage. All of them were carelessly dressed, though to judge from the expression on their faces, their bearing, the cut of their beards, and many almost imperceptible little details, they obviously belonged to the upper classes. (*T*, 63)

The poorly constructed waiting room in *The Trial* is even a step down from the shabby civil environments in Dostoyevski[1] where petitioners await their fates. The great irony here is how poor the dividers of space, light, and air are, despite the power the Law exercises in matters of class, status, and privilege. Like other social-power sources in Kafka's writing such as the Castle hierarchy, the Law's force does not undo the ineptness of its workings and installations, a point hilariously brought home by means of Huld's description of the lawyer's room:

To give only one more example of the state the place was in— there had been for more than a year now a hole in the floor, not so big that you could fall through the floor, but big enough to let a man's leg slip through. The lawyer's room was in the very top attic, so that if you stumbled through the hole your leg hung down into the lower attic, into the very corridor where the clients had to wait. It wasn't saying too much if the lawyers called these conditions scandalous. Complaints to the authorities had not the slightest effect, and it was strictly forbidden for the lawyers to make any structural repairs or alterations at their own expense. Still, there was some justification for this attitude on the part of the authorities. They wanted to eliminate defending counsel as much as possible; the whole onus of the Defense must be laid on the accused himself. (*T*, 116)

If the Court's physical facilities are any indication, the Law is that which exists to violate as well as to assert its boundaries; to withdraw the criteria and mores it has asserted; even to undermine the exaggerated seriousness of its imperatives.

Within the labyrinth of involuted passageways and broken-down stairwells, the atmosphere, for reasons suggested above, is nothing short of oppressive to the newcomer:

> And at the end of the passage now stood the man whom K. had noticed before in the distance; he was holding on to the lintel of the low doorway and rocking lightly on his toes, like an eager spectator. But the girl was the first to see that K.'s behavior was really caused by a slight feeling of faintness; she produced a chair and asked: "Won't you sit down?" K. sat down at once and leaned his elbows on the arms of the chair so as to support himself still more securely. "You feel a little dizzy, don't you?" she asked. . . . "Don't worry," she said. "That's nothing out of the common here, almost everybody has an attack of that kind the first time they come here. This is your first visit? Well, then, it's nothing to be surprised at. The sun beats on the roof here and the hot roof-beams make the air stuffy and heavy. That makes this place not particularly suitable for offices, in spite of the other great advantages it has. But the air, well, on days when there's a great number of clients to be attended to, and that's almost every day, it's hardly breathable. . . . But in the end one gets quite used to it. By the time you've come back once or twice you'll hardly notice how oppressive it is here. Do you really feel better now?" (*T*, 67–68)

This passage details the physical dimensions of the Kafkan protagonist's "seasickness on land,"[2] the imbalance and disorientation produced by the rational man's encounter with the indeterminacy underlying logic and celebrated by art. The Kafkan son is receptive to the Court's corrupt inefficiency, to the obsessive legalistic rumination that would undermine its crude authority; he is drawn to its easy but confused sexuality. But the atmosphere in which the prolonged rumination conducive to this uncertainty takes place is too much for him. At the same time that the Law's female clerical worker rescues him, he is overcome by the shame that, together with his haughtiness, comprises the novel's ongoing affective musical accompaniment, the understated drama explaining the arbitrary and unlikely events.

THE EXCHANGE-HOUSE OF SEXUALITY

The Court atmosphere may not do much to support human life, but it does sustain the activity of relentless legal interpretation, whose behavioral equivalent is an impulsive exchange of sexual partners. The narrative devotes considerable attention to K.'s sexual attitudes, tendencies, and impacts during these early chapters in which he both finds and loses his way amid the Court's installations and complexities. The patterns here established are ones of rapid, spontaneous infatuations; of abandonments every bit as impulsive; of vibrant seductiveness punctuated by repugnant escape from the possessiveness aroused. In *The Trial* as elsewhere in his fiction (notably in *Amerika*) Kafka pays close attention to the hands that are the instruments of physical seduction and the threats of stifling emotional confinement. K. and the Court usher's wife caress each other's hands (*T,* 51); Leni seized "the hand with which K. held her and beginning to play with his fingers" (*T,* 108); K. pushes her "hand away without comment" (*T,* 179) before he undertakes the irreversible move of dismissing his counsel. In between the sexually grasping and off-putting functions served by these hands transpires a volatile economy of sexual exchange and substitution, one that Kafka subtly interjects in the novel by playing on the similarity between the German *tauschen* (to exchange) and *täuschen* (to deceive). So violent is the outbreak of desire and the substitution of sexual objects in *The Trial* that K. can even be captivated (while revolted) by the sadistic punishment scene of chapter 5, whose Whipper "was tanned like a sailor and had a brutal, healthy face" (*T,* 85). In between the time when K., in a passage cited in chapter 5 of this book, literally drinks Fräulein Bürstner in, "like some thirsty animal" (*T,* 29) and when he pushes Leni's hand away, he loses his sexual thirst entirely, and much of his taste for interpersonal relationships.

In a sense, K.'s infatuation with Fräulein Bürstner spans the novel. When he accosts her, the evening after his arrest, his only intimate contacts are "once a week" with "a girl called Elsa, who was on duty all night till early morning as a waitress in a cabaret and during the day received her visitors in bed" (*T,* 17). K.'s fuller-fledged encounters with Fräulein Bürstner/Montag and Leni, which are more akin to flighty dances than love stories, take place in the context of this superficial and stylized heterosexual interaction. When K. is literally herded to his death by two Court henchmen, "before them Fräulein Bürstner appeared, mounting a small flight of steps leading into the square room from a low-lying side-street. . . . Whether it were really Fräulein Bürstner or not, however, did not matter to K.; the important thing was that he suddenly realized the futility of resistance" (*T*, 225). In *The Interpretation of Dreams* and elsewhere, Freud explores the sexual significance of height, falling, and architectural features such as stairways in dreams.[3] Fräulein Bürstner, in this agonizing last vignette we are afforded of her, is more than one particular "ordinary little typist" (*T*, 81). She is heterosexuality itself, or at least K.'s partially realized, partially thwarted relation to it. K.'s last glimpse of her recalls the painful and fatal homeward glance toward normal domesticity cast by Georg Bendemann when he clings to the bridge and beseeches parental love at the end of "The Judgment" and by Gregor Samsa when, as a gigantic dung beetle, he clings to the photograph from his room of a "lady muffled up in so much fur," a final vestige of his personal property (*CS*, 118). Such is the separation-terror that the son of a family, hopelessly embarked on a journey of art, interpretation, and epic or messianic death, experiences.

K.'s interactions with Fräulein Bürstner (whose name is related both to the objects and activity of brushing and to the qualities of unkemptness and resistance), the Court usher's wife, and Leni are playful, spontaneous, whimsical, and spicy. Leni "gave out a bitter exciting odor like pepper" (*T*, 110)—and one of K.'s female acquaintances in *The Castle* will be named Pepi. As suggested above, these infatuations are fueled by, made possible by, K.'s accusation, the stigma of being afoul of the Law, the restraining mode of common human mores. As Lawyer Huld (whose name is but two letters away from *Schuld*, the German word for guilt and obligation) specifies:

"And yet those who are experienced in such matters can pick out one after another all the accused men in the largest of crowds.

How do they know them? you will ask. I'm afraid my answer won't seem satisfactory. They know them because accused men are always the most attractive. It cannot be guilt that makes them attractive, for—it behooves me to say this as a lawyer, at least— they aren't all guilty, and it can't be the justice of the penance laid on them that makes them attractive in anticipation, for they aren't all going to be punished, so it must be the mere charge preferred against them that in some way enhances their attraction. Of course some are much more attractive than others. But they are all attractive, even that wretched creature Block." (T, 184)

Against the backdrop of this intoxicating stigma, K. and his actively sexual partners enter implicit and spontaneous understand-ings, of an irrepressibly erotic nature. This immediate, unstated com-plicity that arises between possible lovers, between partners who have entered each other's allures and made themselves available to one another, remains in many ways the most lasting impression created by these scenes. This complicity forms what the French critic Roland Barthes has called, in a book of the same title, "A Lover's Discourse."[4] " 'You have lovely dark eyes,' she [the Court usher's wife] said, after they had sat down, looking up into K.'s face, 'I've been told that I have lovely eyes too, but yours are far lovelier. I was greatly struck by you as soon as I saw you, the first time you came here. And it was because of you that I slipped later into the courtroom, a thing I never do oth-erwise and which, in a manner of speaking, I am actually forbidden to do'" (T, 52). The aura of transgression itself (a term explored fruitful-ly by the French critic Georges Bataille in his *Histoire de l'érotisme*)[5] enables the Court usher's wife, on the spur of the moment, to cast her inhibitions to the wind and violate her professional job description. Love in Kafka is a dance that brings its partners to the brink. The Kafkan Lover's Discourse gives expression to this brink-dwelling, this inhabiting of the no-person's-land between the Law and utter anarchy. Chancing upon K. does not threaten Leni's job, but it does place her discretion under severe stress.

"But I'm a vain person, too, and very much upset that you don't like me in the least." To this last statement K. replied merely by putting his arm around her and drawing her to him; she leaned her head against his shoulder in silence. But to the rest of her remarks he answered: "What's the man's rank?" "He is an Examining Magistrate," she said. . . . "But must you eternally be brooding over your case?" she queried slowly. "No, not at all," said K. "In fact I probably brood far too little over it." "That isn't the mistake you make," said Leni. "You're too unyielding, that's what I've heard." "Who told you that?" asked K. . . . "Please don't ask me for names," replied Leni, "take my warning to heart instead, and don't be so unyielding in future, you can't fight against this Court, you must confess to guilt." (*T*, 108)

In K.'s sexual encounters, it is always left ambiguous—a threatening situation in a patriarchal society—which partner is taking the initiative. In the above passage Leni offers information and advice with a double freedom: a personal abandon and at no stated cost. Caught up in the allure of marginal mores, Leni places her privileged knowledge at K.'s disposal and at least considers violating Court protocols of secrecy. Though K. is incapable of appreciating it, her performative critique, that he is too unyielding, speaks right to the heart of the matter. It indicates that K. cannot avoid an all-out confrontation with the Law of the Ordinary and the mores of restraint because he is blind to the self-contradictory economy of contempt and shame that dominates him. Leni may not succeed in educating K., in driving home the bits of social savvy he needs in order to strike a compromise with his milieu, but she is most capable of enjoying him. "And if I don't make a confession of guilt, then you can't help me?" K. asks her.

"No," said Leni, shaking her head slowly, "then I can't help you. But you don't in the least want my help, it doesn't matter to you, you're stiff-necked and never will be convinced." After a while she asked: "Have you got a sweetheart?" "No," said K. "Oh, yes, you have," she said. "Well, yes, I have," said K. . . . At her entreaty he showed her Elsa's photograph; she studied it, curled up on his knee. . . . "She's very tightly laced," said Leni, indicating the place where in her opinion the tight lacing was evident. "I don't like her, she's round and clumsy. But perhaps she's soft and kind to you. . . . Big strong girls like that often can't help being soft and kind. . . . Has she any physical defect?" "Any physical defect?" asked K. "Yes," said Leni. "For I have a slight one. Look." She held up her right hand and stretched out the two middle fingers, between which the connecting web of skin reached almost to the top joint, short as the fingers were. In the darkness K. could not make out at once what she wanted to show him, so she took his hand and made him feel it. "What a freak of nature!" said K. and he added, when he had examined the whole hand: "What a pretty little paw!" Leni looked on with a kind of pride while K. in astonishment kept pulling the two fingers apart and then putting them side by side again, until at last he kissed them lightly and let them go. "Oh!" she cried at once. "You have kissed me!" . . . "You have exchanged her for me," she cried over and over again. . . . "You belong to me now," she said.

"Here's the key of the door, come whenever you like," were her last words, and as he took his leave a final aimless kiss landed on his shoulder. (*T*, 109–11)

This passage does not merely record K.'s gain of a sexual open sesame; it demonstrates the dominance of the principles of exchange and substitution over the sexual realm. It also functions as a hub for several of the novel's overall concerns. Leni gleefully detaches K. from the woman she assumes to be his previous commitment. At the same time that she exercises her own will and initiative, she displays a physical defect, a genetic disfiguration, one perhaps reminiscent of an earlier stage of animal evolution. The passage thus links a woman's physical assertion with a physical deformity.

Leni's behavior hints at what her price may be for her various services: possession, defined as a discernible halt along an open-ended sequence of sexual encounters and substitutions. Leni's exclamations underscore her sense of at least temporary dominance over K.'s sexual existence. K. is the designated audience for her performance. It is he who benefits from her joyous sexual expression, her deformity, and her claim. Leni's multifaceted sexual bearing evokes in K. a similarly complex reaction. Leni becomes merely one expression in the novel for K.'s pervasive sexual ambivalence. In very different ways, the similarly volatile Fräulein Bürstner's replacement by the sickly Fräulein

Montag and K.'s fascination with the homoerotically charged whipping scene, are expressive of the same sexual ambivalence, the same hesitation toward direct, unproblematized heterosexual bonding.

It should be noted here that Kafka's intense on-again, off-again romance with Felice Bauer, from August 1912 to Christmas 1917, drained his energies and fueled his imagination considerably, constituting, along with Søren Kierkegaard's broken engagement to Regine Olsen, one of the stormiest liaisons in literary history. Kafka's relationship to Bauer passed from every level of official and unofficial engagement (broken off "officially" at least two times) to every possible expression of unrealistic demand and indifference. In late 1913 and 1914, the struggling relationship was mediated by one Grete Bloch, and there is evidence for speculation concerning Kafka's romantic involvement with the go-between. Block is the name of the burned-out perennial defendant in *The Trial,* while Grete is Gregor Samsa's initially tolerant and compassionate sister in "The Metamorphosis."

The murky underside of the impetuous, spicy love-play K. will engage in with Fräulein Bürstner, the (forever nameless) Court usher's wife, and Leni emerges with particular force in chapter 4, where a sickly and pained Fräulein Montag literally steps into Fräulein Bürstner's place. Fräulein Montag, whose name means Monday, in a sense "the day after," speaks in a style of strained correction. Her language is interspersed with formalistic qualifications. Her intercession on behalf of Fräulein Bürstner amounts to a bucket of cold water thrown upon the seething coals of K.'s arousal. Fräulein Montag is an emissary impeding his reception into the utopia of good sex, the sexual forerunner to the Doorkeeper who will bar entry into the fascinating domain of the Law.

> "I've been asked by my friend to say something to you, that's all. She wanted to come herself, but she is feeling a little unwell today. . . .
>
> "Well, what is there to say?" replied K., who was weary of seeing Fräulein Montag staring so fixedly at his lips. Her stare was already trying to dominate any words he might utter.

"Fräulein Bürstner evidently refuses to grant me the personal interview I asked for." "That is so," said Fräulein Montag, "or rather that isn't it at all, you put it much too harshly. Surely, in general, interviews are neither deliberately accepted nor refused." (*T*, 79)

Fräulein Montag followed him for a few steps as if she did not quite trust him. But at the door they had both to draw back, for it opened and Captain Lanz entered. This was the first time that K. had seen him close at hand. He was a tall man in the early forties with a tanned, fleshy face. He made a slight bow which included K. as well as Fräulein Montag, then went up to her and respectfully kissed her hand. His movements were easy. His politeness toward Fräulein Montag was in striking contrast to the treatment which she had received from K. (*T*, 80)

Not only do the person and manner of Fräulein Montag put a crimp in K.'s evanescent sexuality; in the figure of Captain Lanz he catches a glimpse of his own replacement through the revolving door of romance and apartment occupancy. Although K. has made Lanz's name an occasion for parody at the Court of Inquiry (chapter 2), the character is a more stable and polished sort than K. Not only does a painful substitute for Fräulein Bürstner appear on the menu; K. must address a straitlaced version of himself, a vision of himself as a staid, settled, not overly artistic member of society. Leni's later observation, based on a photograph, that showgirl Elsa is too prudish for K. will be a hilarious elaboration upon the confrontation between conventional and stigmatized, artistic, "accused" versions of himself.

In light of this at-best strained encounter with Fräulein Montag, is it any surprise that K. could demonstrate some fascination with a sadomasochistic scene of outrageous brutality that erupts within the seemingly neutral surroundings of his bank? His muckraking criticisms before the Examining Magistrate have had some effect, it seems. His warders, Franz and Willem, are to be punished for their petty corruption in appropriating his underwear and eating his breakfast. The venue chosen for the punishment is a shocking one for K. It is a storage room in the bank where he works. This eventuality is most disquieting because it means that henceforth there can be no separation of Joseph K.'s trial, hitherto a submerged or "secret" life, on the order of some moderately compromising vice, from his "real" life. The Court penetrates when and where it wishes. The trial, no longer a bizarre exception within the rhythm of a normal, simple life, has become coterminous with that life. The trial exists everywhere Joseph K. does. As a limit of subliminal static or interference to his thought and practical functions, the trial has erupted everywhere. Subsequent attempts to camouflage, repress, or explain it away will prove futile, as will K.'s claim at the end of chapter 5 that the noise from the whipping scene "was only a dog howling in the courtyard" (*T*, 87).

The whipping scene takes place in a closet. The trial is thus of the order of some perverse activity needing to be closeted. The novel, by giving the scene obvious homosexual overtones, does not establish homosexuality as the "true" sexuality for which Joseph K. yearns or as the "hidden" truth of sexual ambivalence. The scenario does, however, make a strong connection between the psychic interference and subliminal insight occasioned by the artist-son's inherited calling and the stigma, dissimulation, and hypocrisy surrounding these acts and tendencies that society brands as morally reprehensible.

Hearing "convulsive sighs behind a door, which he had always taken to be a lumber-room," K., having stayed at work, discovers his warders Franz and Willem under the charge of the brutally handsome Whipper. When K. asks his acquaintances about their purpose ("Was treibt ihr hier?—literally, "What drives you here?") he employs the same verb that serves as the basis of the Freudian *Trieb*, the drive behind all human desires and hungers. This choice of words, together with the warders' presumed rights to their charges' "body-linen," K.'s fascination with "the switch [*Rute*], which the man waved to and fro in front of him" (*T*, 85), and the attention paid to the Whipper's suntan and healthy features, combine to give the scene an undeniable homosexual cast. At the time the scene takes place, it functions as an impediment separating the warder from his fiancée: "My poor sweetheart is waiting the outcome at the door of the Bank. I'm so ashamed and miserable" (*T*, 86–87). Such theft goes on, explains Willem, because the warders are chronically underpaid.

"Franz here wants to get married, a man tries to make whatever he can, and you don't get rich on hard work, not even if you work day and night. Your fine shirts were a temptation, of course that kind of thing is forbidden to warders, it was wrong, but it's a tradition that body-linen is the warders' perquisite, it has always been the case, believe me." (*T*, 84)

Franz in the novel suffers a reversal of his marriage plans as the result of a nasty (but conventional) habit on his part, stealing male underwear, at the same time that Franz Kafka, a man of abrupt liaisons and broken engagements, writes a novel in which his protagonist increasingly falls under the sway of "interference" issuing from a trial that has become his subliminal "second life." The whipping scene of chapter 5 is a turning point in the novel because afterward all of the trial's various forms of static—bureaucratic, interpersonal, sexual—are in place; for better or for worse, K. has found his bearings. In its wake, K.'s rationality and control over his circumstances are at a loss, except in those dimensions in which he becomes alive to the complexities of artistic production and literary interpretation. It is impossible to read this scene, however, in blindness to its unmistakable homoerotic thrust and without understanding the scene's substitutive, supplementary relationship to the novel's heterosexual economy and possibilities. No sooner did Freud, writing his major works contemporaneously with Kafka's, discover and insist upon the decisive influence of sexuality upon human physical and mental health, than he understood the ambivalent, alternating nature of sexual desire. Freud and major literary modernists including Kafka, Proust, Stein, and Joyce were forced to admit the bisexual dimension of the sexual imagination at the same time that they revealed the hidden sexual dimension behind so much behavior and cultural activity. Artistic sensibility is the repressed facet of the commonsense approach to human life in much the same way that homoerotic desire, even where unstated, hovers at the edges of even the most conventional romantic love. In this light, Joseph K.'s trial becomes a perversion, a secret life, a double existence eventually attaining the same status as his "normal" life and overreaching it. We would suffer this effacement as a total loss were it not for the fact that between the lives, between the secret and the explicit, the shameful and the contemptuous, emerge the lineaments and dynamics of artistic production and interpretative insight that transform execution by the Law into a creative triumph. It is to these defiant artistic and interpretative qualities of the Law that we turn as we explore chapters 6–8.

7

The Society of Withdrawal

It is in keeping with the hypothetical nature of Kafka's art that his novels, above all *The Trial* and *The Castle,* become more freewheeling and less structured as they reach toward their (always abrupt) endings. *The Trial,* once it establishes Joseph K.'s predicament, shifts its attention to questions that no novel will ever resolve, but that it, however tentatively, insists upon exploring: What is the nature of the artwork? In what sense is interpretation indispensable to its dynamics? What are the final relationships between the artist's work and his or her life, between fiction and thought, between the laws of fiction and those of the mind (psychology)? Lawyer Huld's diatribes and Titorelli's long-winded explanations in chapter 7 do little to further the novel's plot, but they are essential to an understanding of K.'s legacy and the sensibility that he achieves before meeting his uncanny but ultimately incidental death.

THE INTERPERSONAL VOID

K. hears the Parable of the Doorkeeper, his true sentence, alone in the presence of the priest who is his final judge, and he meets his executioners as a solitary citizen who has known implicitly to dress solemnly for their arrival. ("So you are meant for me?," he asks them when they appear at his lodging on the eve of his thirty-first birthday [*T*, 223], echoing the Doorkeeper's paradox, "No one but you could gain admittance through this door, since this door was intended for you" [*T*, 214–15]). The last time the novel depicts Joseph K. as a member of society, Block's shell-shocked antics alternate with his own clumsy efforts to dismiss his lawyer and reject Leni, the last woman with whom he shares some vestige of active desire (chapter 8).

The novel endows K.'s solitude, whether we think of it as the artist's splendid isolation or the martyr's fate to be misunderstood by his fellow man, with a tragic aura; yet a closer reading of the novel suggests that his loneliness is systematic, a perfectly logical conclusion to the pattern of interpersonal interactions that the narrative has established with care beginning in chapter 1. I have already suggested, in the analysis of chapter 1, that K.'s solitude cannot be understood in isolation from his prevailing emotional economy of contempt and shame. Wherever he goes—his own lodgings, the Court offices, the bank—he undergoes abrupt swings in his attitude from superiority and contempt toward his surroundings and the people he encounters to an intense concern regarding the correctness of his behavior, and above all, about the light in which he is seen. While vibrant and informative, these seemingly antithetical emotions are not conducive to the maintenance of stable friendships or romantic relationships. As Kafka understood, and contemporary depth psychology understands, the antithetical bearings of contempt and shame collapse into a single emotion, or rather scenario, one in which early injuries to the self through an absence of empathy repeat themselves in self-defeating interpersonal relationships.[1] The Court's intrusiveness, the inhumanity of its surroundings, the lack of attention that Huld pays to K. as he delivers his "harangues" (chapter 7, 114–25) are all suggestive of the kind of narcissistic wound that could induce K. to reinforce his loneliness.

In chapters 6–8 the novel elaborates considerably upon K.'s unstable and unsatisfying network of interpersonal relationships. We learn nothing in the novel concerning K.'s "nuclear" family. When his substitute father, Uncle Karl, emerges on the scene in chapter 6, it is with impatience, disapproval of K.'s circumstances, and the intention to take matters under his own control and bring them to the most rapid resolution possible. Like the inevitably misinformed soul in the Parable of the Doorkeeper, Uncle Karl is a *Mann vom Lande,* "a small landowner from the country" (*T,* 91). (He shares these humble origins with most of Franz Kafka's relatives.) He is impulsive, "stretching out his right hand from the very doorway" upon his arrival at K.'s office, "and then thrusting it recklessly across the desk, knocking over everything that came in its way. His uncle was always in a hurry" (*T,* 91). Uncle Karl is the kind of man who wants to take matters quickly and decisively in hand. To this end, he will not hesitate to engage in a bit of guilt-mongering. This is the domestic rather than the legalistic variety of guilt, but it is entirely relevant to K.'s trial. "You don't pay much attention to her," says Uncle Karl, regarding his daughter and K.'s cousin Erna, a boarding-school student who has written him regarding K.'s trial (*T,* 92). Erna has pretended in the letter that K., whose attitude toward the family is one of benign neglect, sent her a box of chocolates for her birthday (*T,* 93).

> "And what have you got to say now?" asked his uncle. . . . "Yes, Uncle," said K., "it's quite true." "True?" cried his uncle. "What is true? How on earth can it be true? What case is this? Not a criminal case, surely?" "A criminal case," answered K. "And you sit there coolly with a criminal case hanging round your neck?" . . . "Joseph, my dear Joseph, think of yourself, think of your relatives, think of our good name. You have been a credit to us until now, you can't become a family disgrace. Your attitude," he looked at K. with his head slightly cocked, "doesn't please me at all, that isn't how an innocent man behaves if he's still in his senses." (*T,* 94)

While Uncle Karl dries a tear off his face prompted by his child's kindness and possibly by K.'s predicament, we cannot quite wipe the smile off our own at the theater tickets K. plans to send to his cousin for "covering" for him with regard to his familial responsibility. To Uncle Karl, K.'s shame and possible guilt are less a matter of any wrongdoing than his indifference to (what Kafka called in a mythical fragment) "the meaningless affair" (*CS,* 432). According to Uncle Karl,

K. is already guilty of this disregard. Not unlike K. himself, Karl's immediate concern is for appearances, family credit, and family disgrace.

K. has indeed been out of touch with his family. He thus joins those loners who seem to abound in modern literature, whether we date this as beginning with Poe's "The Man in the Crowd," Melville's Ishmael, and Dostoyevski's Underground Man, or whether we defer to _ Kafka's protagonists or Camus's *The Stranger*. "Why did you never write to me?" asks Uncle Karl. "You know I would do anything for you, I'm still your guardian in a sense and till now I have been proud of it. Of course I'll do what I can to help you, only it's very difficult when the case is already under way" (*T*, 96). Familial love, as brokered by Uncle Karl, may be a bit begrudging, a bit egocentrically concerned with external appearances, but it is still forthcoming for K. This part of his legacy K. has been only too willing to dispense with. There is a par-ticularly modern humor to his minimal efforts with regard to his cousin. The issue of making fundamental claims upon K.'s duty and good conduct without being able to observe circumstances from his point of view is not such a trivial matter. While Uncle Karl's myopic hustle and bustle add to the novel's comic relief, the same tendency on the part of Lawyer Huld to totally disregard K.'s feelings and contri-butions to his own defense is experienced by K. as so aversive that he eventually abandons his legal battle.

If K.'s contact with his family has been at best passable, his rela-tionships at work have varied from underlying to explicit competitive-ness. The narrative has already betrayed K.'s estimation of the bank clerks who participate in his arrest: "three insignificant anemic young men" (*T*, 15); before the Court of Inquiry in chapter 2, K. identifies Rabensteiner, Kullich, and Kaminer as "three minor employees of my Bank" (*T*, 43). In chapter 7, Kafka goes to considerable efforts to explore the competition between K., the Chief Clerk, and the lesser Assistant Manager, who previously swallowed his pride in order to invite K. on an outing but who now would not mind stepping into his position. Not only does K.'s lagging behind in this commercial race and eventually conceding defeat register the degree of distraction and lassitude emanating from his "second life," the trial, but this development also reveals the underlying ground of ill-will and backbiting that characterizes K.'s work relations.

The narrative is quite explicit about characterizing the interference that the trial has become: "The decision to take his defense into his own hands seemed now more grave to him than he had originally fancied. . . . he would be putting himself completely in the power of the Court. . . . To put up a thoroughgoing defense . . . did that not involve cutting himself off from every other activity? . . . What an obstacle had suddenly arisen to block K.'s career! And this was the moment when he was supposed to work for the Bank?" (*T*, 132–33). K.'s visit from the manufacturer in chapter 7 registers to what degree his Court case has invaded and discombobulated the ordinary affairs of his life. It also becomes an occasion for him and the Assistant Manager to "have it out." "K. had actually followed the man's argument quite closely in its early stages—the thought of such an important piece of business had its attractions for him too—but unfortunately not for too long; he had soon ceased to listen and merely nodded now and then as the manufacturer's claims waxed in enthusiasm, until in the end he forgot to show even that much interest and confined himself to staring at the other's bald head" (*T*, 130). Such is the power of distraction (German *Zerstreutheit*) emanating from the trial at its peak. Kafka's narrative here furnishes an excellent example of the "split consciousness" that Freud isolates as a defining feature of the hysterical neuroses and the uncanny.[2]

In sharp distinction to K., the Assistant Manager is wholly attentive to the discussion. " 'It is a very important proposal,' he said to the manufacturer, 'I entirely agree. And the Chief Clerk'—even in saying this he went on addressing himself only to the manufacturer— 'will I am sure be relieved if we take it off his shoulders. This business needs thinking over. And he seems to be overburdened today.' . . . K. had still enough self-command to turn away from the Assistant Manager and address his friendly but somewhat fixed smile solely to the manufacturer; except for this he did not intervene, supporting himself with both hands on the desk, bending forward a little like an obsequious clerk, and looked on while the two men, still talking away, gathered up the papers and disappeared into the Manager's room" (*T,* 131–32).

The play of substitution does not limit itself to the revolving door of sex. "Smart" money in commerce heeds the call of predatory avarice even if K.'s sexual allure is enhanced by his questionable status, his accusation. Ironically, the Assistant Manager's rapt attentiveness, the lever he uses to displace K. from his accounts, has been character-istic of certain of Kafka's artistic paragons, such as the hunger and trapeze artists. The ultimate pathos of this episode is its sense that even K.'s distracted and partial attention, the most he can muster, is merely a way station in a trajectory inevitably leading to complete functional and psychological derangement. The passivity and dejection to which K. has been reduced in this episode are inconsistent with artistic inten-sity; yet already in this chapter and beyond, K. is launched upon his bizarre countereducation in the ways of texts (legal and fictive) and their interpretation.

K.'s connections to his family have lapsed. His place at work has become a war zone of opposed initiatives and levels of energy. "Gentlemen," the Assistant Manager tells the three other clients who "have already been waiting a long time" and "could no longer be held in check," "there is a very simple solution. If you will accept me, I will gladly place myself at your disposal instead of the Chief Clerk. Your business must, of course, be attended to at once" (*T,* 139). Attention is indeed the issue here: the Assistant Manager has it; K. no longer does, at least for these sorts of things. It is against the backdrop of waning attention, unempathic associations, and fragile self-esteem that we can understand the displays of K.'s haughtiness throughout the novel, for example, in his detachment from the petitioners in the Court offices (*T,* 63–65) and in his disapproval of the Court surroundings (*T,* 51, 53, 59). The novel will reduce K. to the status of Tradesman Block, the Law's most mystified, shell-shocked, perpetual ward, but it will subject him to the even greater humiliation of vying with this legal dis-aster case for Huld's favor.

It is in the pronouncements of Lawyer Huld, to whom K. is taken by his irate uncle, that the Discourse of the Law achieves its full dimensions: a meandering commentary changing hands from character to character as much on the nature of art and interpretation as about the Court. Already K. has witnessed glimmerings of this discourse in his arresting officers' paradoxes and in the advice furnished by the Court usher, his wife, and the girl in the Court offices. Its most significant exponents will be, in addition to Huld, Titorelli, a shattered Block, and ultimately the priest who elucidates the Parable of the Doorkeeper. But for all of Huld's erudition and amusement, he extends the desolate landscape of K.'s interpersonal interactions. K. experiences his long discourses on the complexities and uncertainties of his case as self-important displays of virtuosity relegating him to the far outer reaches of concern. First Uncle Karl and now Huld, his professional extension, ignore K., from his point of view, all the while ostensibly taking up his cause. (In this regard, Gregor Samsa's metamorphosis into a dung beetle cannot be divorced from his family's indifference to his considerable efforts on its behalf, even if no "causal" relationship between the two phenomena can be found. See *CS*, 111.)

> In such and similar harangues K.'s lawyer was inexhaustible. He reiterated them every time K. called on him. Progress had always been made, but the nature of the progress could never be divulged. The lawyer was always working away at the first plea, but it had never reached a conclusion, which at the next visit turned out to be an advantage, since the last few days would have been very inauspicious for handing it in, a fact which no one could have foreseen. . . . The lawyer sipped [his tea], K. squeezed Leni's hand, and sometimes Leni ventured to caress his hair. "Are you still here?" the lawyer would ask, after he had finished. "I wanted to take the tea tray away," Leni would answer, there would follow a last handclasp, the lawyer would wipe his mouth and begin again with new energy to harangue K. (*T*, 124–25)

Huld, like the Court he disputes and represents, and like language itself, is "inexhaustible." A divided K. is sundered between demoralization at Huld's seeming indifference and fascination at the complexity of his legal affair. In his indifference to K.'s reactions and emotions,

Huld becomes a human embodiment of the Court's stifling yet unresponsive atmosphere.

If K. looks longingly backward to Fräulein Bürstner (or someone like her) as he is herded to his death, in Tradesman Block he encounters someone who very much resembles his future state if he persists in his legal defense (Block has sustained his for five years). Block is even *more* distracted, *more* susceptible to superstitions and other hearsay, and *more* ambivalent and unsteady in his relationships than K. is. Block, like a writer or literary scholar, intensifies the torment of living in a textual, interpretative domain while being held to codes of manners, civility, and consistency. Block embodies one very good reason why K., in chapter 10, after minimal resistance, accepts his executioners and his pending death. Death is in some sense preferable to the schism between artistic fascination and a cold and unsympathetic human environment. As contrived and high-blown as the artist-son's martyrdom may be, K. chooses it to the purgatory of evolving into Block. Since Block is an extension of the Kafkan human void, I will close this survey of K.'s interpersonal interactions with him, although he will also figure in K.'s orientation into the despair and joy of commentary.

K.'s encounter with Block is interspersed with K.'s fatal resolve, in chapter 8, to dismiss Huld. The travesty of this interaction serves as a sideshow (or more appropriately dumb show) to the plot's resolution, a musical counterpoint to a fateful event. Throughout the novel there has been an awareness that whatever a trial may be, one's best strategy in surviving it is to stay close to one's friends, to remain embedded in one's network of social relationships however one is tempted to cut loose from it. K. himself has advised the Court usher's wife to "Keep your friendship with these people" (*T*, 53). Huld's fundamental notion of legal activity is the careful nurturing and maintenance of a network of social associations with the judges and other legal personnel out of which, after slow processes of mediation and consensus, the desired result may emerge. "The most important thing," he stresses, "was counsel's personal connection with officials of the Court; in that lay the chief value of the Defense" (*T*, 117). The situation to avoid at all cost is when "The case and the accused and everything were simply withdrawn from the lawyer; then even the best connections with officials would no longer achieve any result, for even they knew nothing" (*T,* 123). Even Block, for all the "pettifogging lawyers" (*T,* 173) he employs on the side in his intense twitchiness, concurs with Huld on this point: "the only pointless thing is to try taking independent action" (*T,* 175). To withdraw one's defense is not merely a legal maneuver; it is to lose irreversibly one's faith in one's human environment, one's social context. Yet this is precisely the move K. is bent upon making when he meets Block, and in its antinomian logic, the novel will even suggest a sense in which this action is a wise and noble one.

" 'So many people seem to be connected to the Court!' said K. with a bowed head," when the manufacturer he disappoints because of his distraction recommends visiting Court painter Titorelli to him (*T,* 135). What is it, exactly, to be on trial, to fight out a case? As suggested above, in the novel's constitutional receptiveness to so many varieties of interpretations, it never precisely answers this question. As the novel progresses, K. learns that he is far from alone in fighting a case. The narrative does tell us that being on trial saps one's energies in leading one's everyday life. It is accompanied by certain psychological symptoms of disorientation, distraction, anxiety, and depression. It results in, and may already be predicated by, damage to one's interpersonal relations. As the novel develops, being on trial expands from a condition specific to the character Joseph K. into a very human attribute, and its remedy appears more and more in the form of common wisdom, the legacy of unofficial knowledge passed from generation to generation.

The wisdom that K. gains in the course of the novel, only to ignore it, may be summarized as follows: you are not alone in experiencing the splitting, doubt, and torment of human consciousness. As Titorelli will explain in detail, you will not obtain any simple or definitive relief from this burden, but there are options (that he calls ostensible acquittal and postponement) under which you can survive. Survival above all demands that you keep your faith with your fellow human beings and maintain a healthy, vibrant set of human relationships.

But K. will not heed this advice. He is too much of an interpreter, if not an artist, and the nourishment of human relationships (as
in "A Hunger Artist") does not sustain him. His interaction with Block
devolves into childlike games of betrayal. While K. receives Block's
disclosure that he employs "pettifogging lawyers" and keeps this confidence, Block, K.'s future emanation, publicizes the secret that K.
shares in turn, that he intends to dismiss Huld, almost before K. has
enunciated it (*T*, 182). Block's imitation of a dog at Huld's request (*T*,
191–93) not only indicates the attorney's power over him: it suggests
the degree to which he has devolved in conducting his defense with
"good sense."

In relinquishing his will to live, K. also abandons the contempt
upon which he has drawn to conduct his interpersonal affairs: "The
contempt which he had once felt for the case no longer obtained. Had
he stood alone in the world he could have easily ridiculed the whole
affair, though it was also certain that in that event it could never have
arisen at all" (*T*, 126). Life itself is tantamount to the pride, egotism,
and vacillation between contempt and shame with which we negotiate
our everyday affairs, the errors of conscience which become the
grounds for our personal trials. To view life through the eyes of the
artist and the interpreter is a way of circumventing, possibly tran-
scending, this egotism; unfortunately, it is also a way of terminating
life. This is the Paradox of Paradoxes that K. discovers, the one that
the novel never resolves.

At one turn in the novel's surrealistic afterlife, "The End" (chapter 10), K. "suddenly realized the futility of resistance. There would be
nothing heroic in it were he to resist, to make difficulties for his companions, to snatch at the last appearance of life by struggling. He set
himself in motion and the relief his warders felt was transmitted to
some extent even to himself" (*T*, 225). K.'s henchmen become his
"companions" just after he catches a final glimpse of Fräulein Bürstner.
In its interpretative multiplicity, *The Trial* furnishes one respect in
which K.'s bizarre, chosen, and to some extent self-administered death —
"makes sense." K.'s demise may fly in the face of the conventional wisdom, but it comprises one moment in the novel when he is in step (literally) with his companions, when he triumphs over the divisive,

competitive impacts of authority and conventional striving. The relief that the henchmen feel at K.'s relinquishment of his conventional egotism, even his will to live, is transmitted back to K. An absurdity. But in one sense, in the context of the interpersonal interactions to which the narrative devotes considerable attention and detail, K. has achieved a certain solidarity with his compatriots that has previously eluded him, a liberation from the progressively isolating demands of narcissistic contempt and shame. He achieves this liberation, and consciously faces death, on the basis of the insight into art and interpretation with which such characters as Huld, Titorelli, and even Block furnish him. It is to this interpretative knowledge, wisdom from the perspective of art rather than normality or survival, that we now turn.

"THIS GREAT ORGANIZATION . . . IN A STATE OF DELICATE BALANCE"

What can a fictive surrogate who progressively loses his associates, his sexual appetite, and his capacity to work be said to gain? The answer to this question must remain very close to the Court which is also the setting for K.'s demise. In fact, knowledge of the Court, as an encompassing literary domain operating according to principles of association, opposition, displacement, derangement, and paradox—as elucidated by its various servants, lawyers, victims, Titorelli, and the priest—is precisely what K. gains in the course of the novel. K. accrues his knowledge of the Law and the literary text by exposure; and through his or her exposure to K., the reader witnesses one of the great disclosures and dramatizations of its own internal workings that literature has ever offered.

"The right perception of any matter and a misunderstanding of the same matter do not wholly exclude each other," qualifies the priest in his elucidation of the Parable of the Doorkeeper (*T*, 216). This enigmatic tale, narrated to K. after he has taken the fatal but resolute step of dismissing his counsel, not only situates interpretation at the heart and crux of literary creativity and understanding, but it also reveals the sequence of interpretations that have structured K.'s trajectory. Knowledge, as it may be extrapolated from the Parable of the Doorkeeper, consists of the collision and reverberations between versions of the same story. Each understanding of the riddle is itself fragmentary, incomplete, distorted, and biased; knowledge, such as we can attain it, consists in the generation of meanings dissonant and imperfect in themselves, but achieving coherence under the vigilant eye of interpretation.

K.'s experience throughout the novel transpires within the scenario of the Parable. This experience, confining itself within the parameters of the vast, self-contradictory, and self-effacing image of the Court, proceeds through a gathering of legal interpretations from a wide range of sources. As we have begun to see, the interpretations to which K. is exposed are at times apocryphal, mystifying, deluded, hilarious, and deadly accurate. The lesson, what K. truly gathers from the bizarre sequence of events, is in the dynamics of interpretation, the interplay between the imperfect renditions, the processes of illumination and disqualification by which the drafts of understanding are linked.

The Court is the imposing and ponderous image within whose boundaries the unfolding and drama of interpretation transpires. It was Kafka's tendency in the novels to confine his protagonists' discoveries and sufferings to the possibilities released through the unfolding of a single, highly complex image. This image, whether the Court, the Castle, or the vast terrain of America, is oppressive in its prevalence and its extension, but the disclosure of the complexity within its ponderous presence becomes the ultimate source of release and hope in Kafka's writing. It is as if Kafka subordinated his major projects to the gravitational pull of images possessing the mass, vitality, and authority that he associated with Hermann Kafka, only to record the dissolution of this control through the generation and proliferation of imaginative possibilities. The gullible and ineffectual man from the country may ultimately be thwarted in his efforts to gain entry into the awesome domain of the Law, but through K. and in full cognizance of his sufferings, Franz Kafka succeeds in opening the vibrant and multifaceted domain of literature to his readers. This is the fullest redemption that the artist-son can imagine and deliver, as close to redemption as literature strays. Its personal cost, its martyrdom, as assessed in *The Trial* and elsewhere, is measured in enduring wounds, thwarted relationships, and overbearing senses of emptiness and meaninglessness.

Huld's role in the exchange of legal opinions staged by the novel is to stress the Court's vastness, the insignificance of any single opinion or volition to its magisterial deliberations. The narrative, taking on his point of view (as happens, with characters in the bureaucratic sections near the ends of both *The Trial* and *The Castle*), describes his vision of the Court in this way: "The ranks of officials in this judiciary system mounted endlessly, so that not even the initiated could survey the hierarchy as a whole. And the proceedings of the Courts were generally kept secret from subordinate officials" (*T*, 119). It falls upon Huld's incapacitated shoulders to introduce the vision of the Court as an infinite regression, a panorama of interlocked but poorly connected levels in which communications are particularly apt to get lost, and in which entire legal procedures, by virtue of this oblivion, must be repeated over and over again. Huld thus heralds the glimpse of the Law that the man from the country will be allowed in the recounting of the Parable that K. hears: "From hall to hall, keepers stand at every door, one more powerful than the others. And the sight of the third man is already more than even I can stand" (*T*, 213). The immensity of the interpretative space demanded by the Court is the domesticated, contemporary version of the construction project that Kafka elaborated in "The Great Wall of China," with all the breaches, time lags, and temporal absurdities that it occasioned (see *CS*, 235, 238, 243–44). While the emotive correlative to this immense, layered landscape of commentary and bureaucratic deliberation may well be a chilling indifference, the setting also allows for humor, to wit, Huld's amusing tale of the beleaguered official who manages to throw every lawyer mounting to see him down the stairs until the lawyers band together and wear him out (*T*, 120–21).

While the edifice of the Law is so grandiose and has so many checks and balances built into it that it is, in effect, "earthquake proof" and can never topple, the footing inside it is treacherous for any individual. The need for a cautious, team approach to the Court's innumerable pitfalls is the crux of Huld's message:

> One must lie low, no matter how much it went against the grain, and try to understand that this great organization remained, so to speak, in a state of delicate balance, and that if someone took it upon himself to alter the disposition of things around him, he ran the risk of losing his footing and falling to destruction, while the organization would simply right itself by some compensating reaction in another part of its machinery—since everything interlocked—and remain unchanged, unless, indeed, which was very probable, it became still more rigid, more vigilant, severer, and more ruthless. One must really leave the lawyers to do their work, instead of interfering with them. (*T*, 121)

In such a passage Kafka gives us glimpses of the image that he sketches in his fragments and parables and that he allows himself to paint in large scale in the novels. What is this image of? We may take it, like social critics, tangibly, as an impression of the immensity and confusion of twentieth-century administrative life. Or, in a more theoretical vein, we may approach this vision of stately equilibrium and interlocking in the face of daily buffeting as a rendition of a particular language user's encounter with the pliable but ultimately impersonal system of language by which she or he expresses herself or himself. Like the Law, language enters the most private and intimate domains of our existence. It is the only medium available to us for expressing, even conceptualizing, our most basic apprehensions and desires. Yet as "immediate," as "natural" as this communications medium is to us, certain of its facets remain beyond our control, impersonal, impervious to our feelings and wishes. As individuals, for example, we do not determine language's internal rules or Law: its syntax and its grammar. Freud defined the uncanny as the strangeness capable of overcoming the most familiar.[3] There is something congenitally uncanny about language and the manner by which it bridges the most familiar references to a code of overarching, impersonal laws, and no literary artist has ever been more acute than Kafka in sensing and figuring this uncanniness. Through Huld's sage advice, warning K., for practical reasons, to subjugate his particular whims and desires to the dictates of the Law (whether of the state or language), K. gains an early insight into the impersonal—that is, artistic and linguistic—dimensions of his predicament, which thus loses its pathos as it approaches circumstantial death.

PORTRAITS

It is fully in keeping with my basic understanding of the novel's development—the legacy and sacrifice of art may confuse and ultimately derange the human child's life, but also inform, "riddle" it with insight—that the most exhaustive account of K.'s options is entrusted not to a legal professional but to Court artist Titorelli. It falls upon Titorelli, at the end of chapter 7, to inform K. that any definitive relief from his torment, any absolute "definite" acquittal in his case, is out of the question, unattainable. Conversely, the two forms of acquittal that he might receive, after monomaniacal dedication and self-denial, amount to complementary forms of uncertainty and agonizing doubt. The absolute of definite acquittal relates to the two attainable possibilities as an idealized myth or legend to the facts of reality. " 'Such acquittals,' replied the painter, 'are said to have occurred. Only it is very difficult to prove the fact. . . . All the same, they shouldn't be entirely left out of account, they must have an element of truth in them. . . . I myself have painted several pictures founded on such legends'" (*T*, 154). Of the two *possible* forms of acquittal, the "ostensible" variety is a painfully slow consensus achieved through references and affadavits, whose pitfall, however, is that the procedure, in a tortuous bureaucratic path marked by regular breakdowns in communication and losses of documents, may have to be repeated over and over again (*T*, 157–59). Postponement, on the other hand, "consists in preventing the case from ever getting any further than its first stages" (*T*, 160). The problem with this option is that it demands an attentiveness as punishing as punishment itself (*T*, 161). K.'s indoctrination into the possible outcomes of his case amounts to a presentence or a sentence before the sentence. In practical terms, his options are both diabolical, but they are possessed of a genuinely aesthetic symmetry and irony. Both available " 'methods have this in common, that they prevent the accused from coming up for sentence.' 'But they also prevent an actual acquittal,' said K. in a low voice, as if embarrassed by his own perspicacity'" (*T*, 161–62). In answer to our earlier question about any possible gain accruing from the existential and psychological travail of a trial, K.'s "own perspicacity" must do, one that expands in a most deliberately artistic fashion and environment.

For the importance of K.'s dialogue with Titorelli consists not merely in its *result*, K.'s legal education, but more importantly in its *setting*. Not only do we share with K. glimpses of certain portraits in this scene. In its minutest details, this scene comprises a repetition (as in "ostensible acquittal") and a consolidation of the Court's most telling and creative qualities. As a reassembly and allegory of the novel's own past history and the details of its own performance, the scene in which K. encounters Titorelli constitutes a revelation and critical commentary upon *The Trial*'s own art. This is the sense in which K., in learning the wider implications of his predicament, should interact with an artist in a working atelier. The scene sets *The Trial*'s own artistry in full relief; it constitutes a tour de force of its own performance.

Like other Court installations, Titorelli's atelier is situated in a building that is shoddily constructed, labyrinthine, and poorly lit. The episode incorporates so many features and details to which the text devoted attention in other settings, in a seemingly random fashion, that it epitomizes both the novel's artistic control and K.'s loss of control over his own situation. The close, oppressive, and overbearing qualities of Titorelli's environment extend into the experience of reading these passages. The repetitions out of which this episode configures itself transforms the novel into an intensified, somewhat demonic counterversion of itself. The encounter forces K. to relive the cumulative agony of his experience since the unilateral initiation of the case, that is, since the beginning of the novel.

The little band of intrusive girls that surrounds K. on the stairway to Titorelli's apartment is reminiscent of the "many children" K.

disturbed on his way to his first interrogation "who were playing on the stairs and looked at him angrily as he strode through their ranks" (*T*, 35). The leader of this latter crew is a hunchback, recalling not only the other deformed (female) characters in the novel but the earlier "sickly young girl . . . standing at a pump in her dressing-jacket and gazing at K. while the water poured in her bucket" (*T*, 35). Titorelli's neighborhood is "even poorer," "almost at the diametrically opposite end of the town from the offices of the Court" (*T*, 141), yet the latter setting derives its qualities through comparison with the former. "Beneath the other wing" of Titorelli's tenement "there was a gaping hole of which, just as K. approached, issued a disgusting yellow fluid, steaming hot, from which some rats fled into the adjoining canal" (*T*, 141).

"The air was stifling" in this environment (*T*, 141). Kakfa pays careful attention to architectural features and details of space, atmosphere, and light that also figure in other scenes dispersed throughout the novel. These references function like the tentacles of an octopus, arranging the novel's prior scenes and settings around this one. "This stairway was extremely narrow, very long, without any turning, could thus be surveyed in all its length, and was abruptly terminated by Titorelli's door" (*T*, 142). This crooked stairway leads not only to the Court painter but to every analogous structure in the novel: "the shut wooden staircase" through which Bertold carries the Court usher's wife to the Examining Magistrate (*T*, 59, 61), for example, and the one down which the lawyers are thrown in Huld's anecdote (*T*, 120). K. finds the atmosphere in the atelier "almost unbearable." " 'No,' replied the painter" to his request to open a window, "It's only a sheet of glass let into the roof, it can't be opened. . . . Because it's hermetically sealed it keeps the warmth in better than a double window, though it's only a simple pane of glass. And if I want to air the place . . . the air comes in everywhere through the chinks' " (*T*, 155). This description of course draws us back to the female Court employee's explanation of K.'s faintness in the Court offices (*T*, 67–68). But the encounter with Titorelli is not only linked to K.'s misadventures in the Court installation "almost at the diametrically opposite end of the town" (*T*, 141). The lock and keyhole, for example, around which the unkempt girls crowd (*T*, 145, 148) leads the reader back to the grille in Huld's door, at which Uncle Karl waits so impatiently (*T*, 99).

In surveying K.'s options in this scene, Titorelli will conjure up "an enormous fabric of guilt" (*T*, 149). It is one of K.'s major fictive achievements in the novel—an incisive window into the workings of fiction that he does in fact open—that this episode, in which a litany of the Court's ubiquitous connections arises, attaches itself to many of the most memorable scenes and details in the novel. For purposes of the novel, the meeting with Titorelli becomes its internal Court. "These girls belong to the Court too," explains Titorelli to K. "You see, everything belongs to the Court" (*T*, 150). "Didn't you know that there were Law Court offices here? There are Law Court offices in almost every attic, why should this be an exception?" (*T*, 164). It is a most important innovation of this novel that its *setting*, the offices and installations of the Court, derives its distinctive qualities and dynamics from the organization—the stayings, repetitions, associations, and allusions—of a literary *artist*. In this sense, the Court whose ways K. learns even if the process kills him (the German title of the novel is *Der Prozeß*), *is* a literary text, and K., while a suffering artist and son, learns to be a reader and interpreter of textual complexities.

Titorelli is the Court painter, a hereditary position of another sort. Titorelli is the son of an artist, along with Kafka, another artist-son. Titorelli is a painter, and it is not only within his atelier that paintings in the novel abound. The paintings in the novel serve a multifaceted function. Not only are they artworks, revealing the ironies of power at the same time that they depict their often corrupt and rapacious "subjects." They reflect on the composition of the novel at hand, and they are suggestive of the ways in which Kafka filled his own various types of fictive canvasses.

K. happens upon paintings in three locations: in Huld's apartment (*T*, 107–8), in the artist's atelier, and at the Cathedral where the priest recites and elucidates the Parable of the Doorkeeper for him (*T*, 205). Were we to generalize about the paintings assimilated into the narrative surface of *The Trial*, we would have to say that they are ironic in nature: they reveal an underlying predatory facet to the subjects that they are intended to celebrate, embellish, and legitimate. From the paintings with which Kafka illuminates the mysteries of *The Trial*, we may infer that the painted artwork is above all a medium of subversion through an apparent capitulation to convention. The paintings in *The Trial*, like Titorelli, "do their job." They do it in such a way as to cast light upon their patrons' moral flaws and to give vent to their own anger. The solemn portrait of a judge in Titorelli's atelier is inappropriately painted in pastel colors because, as the painter explains, the "client wished it . . . he intends the picture for a lady" (*T*, 147). While the subject of the painting debases the artistic production by using it as a love trinket, Titorelli gains his revenge by inscribing an extra figure "rising in the middle of the picture from the high back of the chair" in which the judge is enthroned (*T*, 146). It is in the shadow of obscurity that Titorelli achieves his subterfuge.

> This play of shadow bit by bit surrounded the head like a halo or a high mark of distinction. But the figure of Justice was left bright except for an almost imperceptible touch of shadow; that brightness brought the figure sweeping right into the foreground and it no longer suggested the goddess of Justice, or even the goddess of Victory, but looked exactly like a goddess of the Hunt in full cry. The painter's activities absorbed K. against his will. (*T*, 147)

Thus does the idealized personification of Justice devolve, with the help of Titorelli's subversive brushwork, into a predatory Diana. (Note how female archetypes dramatize here the judicial violence acted out by men.) By the same token, an attentive "huge armored knight . . . leaning on his sword, which was stuck into the bare ground" somehow manages to insinuate himself into "the outermost verge" of an otherwise conventional altarpiece painting of Christ's burial in a side chapel of the Cathedral in chapter 9 (*T*, 205). Titorelli's aggressive Justice not only furnishes an accurate but unwanted legend to the enshrined judge's image, it serves as a talisman for an entire art form of critical subversion or subversive conventionality. It remains questionable, however, whether Kafka's literary art could confine itself to such an artistic insignia, or be exhausted by it, even if it underscores an ironic art of debunking. All emblems, even subversive ones, amount to idealizations. For Kafka as well as for Titorelli, the son's ultimate weapon is his art. But Kafka's verbal artwork is so relentless in elaborating the weaknesses and hypocrisies in all the perspectives it incorporates, including the son's, that the emblematic artwork of debunking cannot in the end "do it justice."

The emphasis on painted canvasses in the novel does, however, underscore Kafka's intense awareness of the depth and extent of his own verbal painting. In comparison to the absolute release of "definite acquittal," the available possibilities of "ostensible acquittal" and "postponement" amount to fragments, mere sketches of the big picture. Kafka painted the broad canvasses of novels in part to reveal how inevitably fragmentary this genre is, to belie its pretensions to narrative conformity and completeness. He devoted every bit as much labor and space to admittedly incomplete, marginal genres: fables, parables, diary entries, letters—in part to demonstrate how full and inexhaustible such fragments could be. In this sense, *The Trial,* as well as the other two novels, in a painterly fashion, dramatizes the play of fragment and whole whose most explicit formulation is "The Great Wall of China."

THE COMMENTATOR AND THE DOG

It is impossible to close these comments on the novel's late intermediary chapters without a few remarks concerning Block, K.'s last guide to the Law in the "body" of the novel proper. We have already encountered him in the context of K.'s limited and ultimately unsatisfying interpersonal interactions. Yet his overall relevance to the novel is central, crucial, even though he is quintessentially a character of extremes. Within the multiple sea changes registered by chapter 8, Block emerges as a violently ambivalent figure, reacting even more sensitively than Titorelli to the inconsistencies and paradoxes of the legal code, but at the same time at the mercy of every superstition arising from the Court.

As opposed to Huld and Titorelli, Block derives his understanding of the Court from being one of its victims, not one of its fixtures. On one level, his reading continues the increasing realization of the textual character of the Law marked by Titorelli. But the shattering of his personality, most evident in the violence with which he turns on K. when he suspects him of divulging his secrets to Huld, cannot be divorced from this increasing realization. For Block, the distracted defendant, the trial is retained only within the memory afforded by the transcript he has provided for himself. His most fundamental self-defense has consisted in assuming the function of a scribe: "I have written it down here. I can give you exact dates if you like. It's difficult to keep them in one's head" (T, 172). It is also indicative of Block's interpretative posture to the Law that the labor Huld extracts from him is the study of the legal script. Although Block can only address his trial as a text, his concept of legal language appears both primitive and debased in comparison with the neat determinations according to which Titorelli can categorize K.'s different alternatives.

One of the most striking instances in the novel of K.'s presuppositions being submitted to a violent overturning occurs when Block recapitulates the scene of K.'s first visit to the Court offices, where he, unknown to K., was one of the silent bystanders in the hall. K. assumes that the deference shown by the other defendants for the usher, who accompanies him, is also intended for himself and that the accused take him for an official, "perhaps he actually took him for a Judge," (T, 65). It is in this scene that K. discomposes one of the bystanders by inquiring as to his case and even brings him to the point of hysterical shrieking by touching him with an emphatic gesture. Although this nameless character does admit to knowing that K. is a defendant, K. continues to assume that he is being taken for something else. Block places this scene in a completely different light in his recapitulation.

> "Well, people declared that judging from the expression of your lips you would be found guilty, and in the near future too. I tell you, it's a silly superstition and in most cases completely belied by the facts, but if you live among these people it's difficult to escape the prevailing opinion. You can't imagine what a strong effect

such superstitions have. You spoke to a man up there, didn't you? And he could hardly utter a word in answer. Of course there's many a reason for being bewildered up there, but one of the reasons why he couldn't bring out an answer was the shock he got from looking at your lips. He said afterwards that he saw on your lips the sign [*Zeichen*] of his own condemnation." (*T*, 174)

In this passage, K.'s prior understanding of the scene in the Court offices is completely disqualified, for he learns that instead of asserting his power over the other defendants, he was communicating with them in a language of which they alone possessed mastery, a sublanguage whose signs ("the line of his lips," "the sign") consisted of lip movements independent of the enunciated word. Shattered by the rigidity of the Court's written language, the defendants are afforded some penetration into its workings by means of this subliminal code. The language of the Law widens to encompass even preverbal signs. The context in which this sublanguage arises is the superstition that substitutes (*zum Ersatz*) for any clear notion of Court functioning held by the defendants. The German *Aberglaube*, or "superstition," carries the etymological connotation of "belief in spite of," or belief in what is available to sustain belief. Block's interpretation of the earlier scene carries with it a widening of the notion of language operative in the novel. This semiology extends beyond the written text and incorporates the gesture, voluntary and convulsive. Linguistic competence in this language enables even the most intimidated victims of the law to fabricate fiction. Toward the end of this chapter, where Block's critical distance gives way to a total subservience to Huld as an agent of the Court, the purpose served by this code is demonstrated: "All this time Block's lips were moving unceasingly; he was obviously formulating the answers he hoped Leni would make" (*T*, 194). In the same gesture with which he expresses his utmost terror, Block anticipates Leni's responses in a pantomime and thus, in a sense, invents them.

Block's extratextual perception cannot be divorced from, and indeed is a function of, his subjection to the Law's fictions. Block's susceptibility and sensitivity are not contradictory. The acuity with which he sees through Huld's declarations and proscriptions does not prevent the shattering of his personality, nor does it exclude the possibility of total subjection to Huld. Acuity and knowledge are precisely what block Block's self-mastery. As Huld puts it, imprisonment is often superior to freedom (*T*, 189). A dismembered personality, robbed of its internal coherence, is the context in which Block's intelligence and superstition coincide, a split personality, for he is both the reader who is entirely at the mercy of the Court's fictions and the law's most sensitive exegete. Block straddles the violent gulf between a labored faith and the cynicism of an accomplished reader. His orthodoxy is complemented by his willingness to delve into the Court's most sordid corners. His fate is to suffer the trembling that marks the discrepancy between these extremes, the anxious quaking signaling the vulnerability of the Hegelian slave (but also his or her persistence through labor): "for the fellow now began to tremble in earnest" (*T*, 190).

Even while K.'s "personal" life becomes increasingly disastrous, the exchange of interpretations and aesthetic sensibility that we have now followed through readings furnished by Huld, Titorelli, and Block have become richer and more complex. Any growth or gain that transpires in the novel must be measured in this way. Such a deepening of understanding, whether it accrues to K. or to the reader pursuing his trajectory, is by no means linear or sequential in its development. Each of the interpretive stages followed by the novel is fraught with its own paradoxes and ambiguities. Huld's apparent self-certainty regarding his position within a knowable network of associations near the beginning of the novel will be modified by his fabricating belief-sustaining fictions in the eighth chapter, a tendency being emphasized as the chapter reaches its premature ending. The exteriority afforded by Titorelli's unique position within the Court is belied by the interiority of his commerce with the judges and officials and by the reduction to sameness of the only alternatives he has to offer. In addition, Block's uncanny penetration goes hand in hand with a servile acceptance of all of the Court's fabrications.

In staging an endless and relentlessly self-qualifying exchange of interpretations, *The Trial* will admit of no resting place, no authoritative reader. Its candidate for the register of literary heroism must surely be Block, for he has faced and spanned the novel's duplicity.

8

The Parable of Parables

The Trial is at the same time one of the most compelling masterworks of world literature and one of the crowning documents of human psychology. It achieves psychological veracity at the same time that it epitomizes a literary sensibility and literary thought. It has struck and inspired its readers both as a groundbreaking literary artifact and because it intensifies certain elements of our psychological life whose articulation has not been so precise and moving elsewhere. To apply to K. the epithet by which Joseph Conrad identifies Lord Jim and sets the stage for his ambiguity, K. "was one of us."[1] The distraction, disorientation, alienation, despair, and sense of threat that "he" feels, characterize, at an extreme, perceptions and moods that many of his most responsive readers have shared with "him." It is not accidental, however, that in a artwork so "true to life" we find such intense and technically accurate allegories of literary form, narration, and signification. A sublime understanding of literary detachment, artifice, and distortion coincides with a psychological scenario of near-universal recognizability. The technical understanding of language that makes *The Trial* a literary tour de force coincides with a psychological receptivity to its characters' moods, thought processes, and mental distortions. *The Trial* is not merely an engaging or well-constructed novel: it is a treatise on the nature and operation of literature. It is striking, and somewhat ironic, that the most literary works, those with the most advanced theoretical "operating systems" accounting for their design and substantive particularities, are also those most deeply rooted in a certain psychological "truth."

Nothing could seem to be more antithetical to literature's defiant appeal for and dramatization of freedom, singularity, and incommensurability than the pressing needs and eternal laws of the psyche. In the complex interaction between the psyche and the text, the former plays a role somewhat like the grasping women who, aroused by his culpability, pursue a somewhat inconsistent and shattered K. Yet both the psyche and the text revolve around language. For the psyche, language is the very possibility and means of communication: it is the medium through which all thoughts, feelings, perceptions, and moods are enunciated and transmitted. Self-aware, densely wrought literature, as composed by Kafka, challenges the assumptions upon which intellectual systems, including psychology, rest, but by engaging and improvising upon the same linguistic medium by which the psyche makes itself known to itself. The psyche is the arena in which the artwork, including the literary text, makes itself intelligible, or, as the case may be, incomprehensible; the text (regardless of its formal aesthetic attributes) is the configuration upon which the psyche leaves its imprint; is the medium through which the psyche will discover, by means of radical distortions, the submerged facets of itself.

Contemporary psychologists of the self have described introspection as the delving toward an integration of archaic versions or drafts of the self with its latest, partially rational, partially flawed, contemporary descendant.[2] The impact of writers, by the same token, especially those who trigger profound intellectual recrystallizations on the part of their contemporary and subsequent readers, may be described as a critical reintegration of segments of the cultural landscape that have gotten out of synch with one another, that have gone "incommunicado." The writer's journey is an engagement with the facets of individual and collective awareness that have become fragmented and submerged. The disclosures that become manifest to the writer in the process of writing, may, under the proper cultural circumstances, achieve a form enabling a reintegration of fragmented awareness on the part of its readers. Writing, thus, in its multiple forms—its pictorial, plastic, musical, philosophical, and scientific, as well as its literary notations—is a psychoanalytical process, whose cultural impact becomes integration or reintegration. And criticism becomes an ongoing vehement struggle to resist the forgetting, cultural repression, and segmentation of awareness that emerge with time and for purposes of political, disciplinary, and ideological expediency.

This discussion of *The Trial*'s impact in the broadest terms—in terms, by the way, through which we may understand the importance of all artifacts that are both remembered and that continue to inspire informed and vibrant commentary—coincides with my survey of the novel's two final chapters for good reasons. In the final two chapters K. wanders as close to any "truth" or final revelation that the novel is going to put forward; and he is executed, in a fashion whose polite manners and cultivated setting will belie the violence of the act. The form of the novel's ultimate revelation—in keeping with a story in which K.'s only gain has consisted of an education in the ambivalence and indeterminacy of language and its artifacts—is a striking but entirely inconclusive and fragmentary parable. The Parable of the Doorkeeper explicitly formulates and dramatizes the grounds for the novel's compelling nature and its operating principles. It opens an ambiguity—whether the "man from the country" deluded himself by spending a lifetime at the entrance to the Law—receptive to a vast and possibly overwhelming range of interpretations and points of view. Like *The Trial* itself, the Parable of the Doorkeeper solicits and inspires a full range of its readers' reactions and awareness. It must finally be inconclusive, like *The Trial* itself, but in its *process* it has achieved the reintegration that is literature's response and defiance to the tragedy of human existence.

Needless to say, the episode in which the Parable is read to K. and interpreted for him in chapter 9 and our assimilation of that episode impact upon our understanding of the execution scene in "The End." Is K. executed by some cruel and inhuman authority, or does he, despite some initial hesitation, face his death, a death in both existential and artistic terms, with bravery and defiance? Or does some strange logic exist that would sustain both of these seemingly antithet-ical understandings? The Parable of the Doorkeeper furnishes the final, if not highest, resolution the novel can offer to the anomalies and ambiguities that characterize the Law; yet it too is a mystery, a bot-tomless enigma. If it is incumbent upon the Parable of the Doorkeeper to *resolve* the novel, to justify it, to infuse it with "higher" meaning, it might seem that Joseph K.'s explorations and efforts have come to naught, that his death is comprehensible only as an ominous moral outrage issuing from some cloaked source. But if we read the Parable as *intensifying* the aesthetic sensibility that has become K.'s acquired legacy, if not a birthright, there may be a sense in which his execution is also an embrace of the negativity that art has symbolized and demonstrated throughout the novel.

An undisclosed amount of time has passed since K. dismissed Huld and the lawyer's approach to salvaging his customary life. K. is summoned to the Cathedral where he will hear the Parable by means of a pretext that is not without its own interest. After concluding a short business trip (of the type on which Franz Kafka was often sent to provincial factories), K. is to show "An Italian colleague, who was on his first visit to the town and was one of the Bank's most influential clients, . . . some of the town's art treasures and monuments" (*T*, 197). K. is chosen for this mission not only because of an "at least adequate" knowledge of Italian, but because of the fact, as the novel at this very late stage reveals, "he had some knowledge of art, acquired in earlier days, which was absurdly overestimated in the Bank owing to his hav-ing been, for some time, purely as a matter of business, a member of the Society for the Preservation of Ancient Monuments. Rumor had it that the Italian was also a connoisseur" (*T*, 199). Whether "purely as a matter of business" or not, K. does have some predilection for art in his background. Art, then, is what summons him to the Cathedral where he will learn the novel's final but fragmentary lesson: one that is at the same time moral and artistic and an insight into the human psy-che. In deference to the Parable's constitutional incompleteness, the novel tarries before sending K. to this fateful encounter. The narrative explores the ambiguous altar painting in the Cathedral's side chapel (*T*, 205), and it goes over the Italian visitor's suspicious characteristics:

the incomprehensible local dialect into which he lapses (*T*, 200), and his "obviously perfumed" mustache that tempts K. "to go close up and have a sniff at it" (*T*, 200)—perhaps a reprise of the novel's underlying current of homoerotic interest.

The path leading K. to the Parable is an indirect one. Substituting for the no-show Italian businessman (in a fashion recalling Fräulein Montag's earlier role as stand-in for her sexually volatile friend), a mysterious limping verger in the background "started pointing with his right hand . . . in some vaguely indicated direction" (*T*, 206) and then points to a priest. The verger's gesture is reminiscent of Block's spasmodic sign language. Once again K.'s assumption of the mediocrity around him submits to a revision. "Perhaps the verger was not such an imbecile after all and had been trying to urge K. toward the preacher, a highly necessary action in that deserted building" (*T*, 207).

The preliminaries over, K. and the reader are prepared for the narration of the Parable of the Doorkeeper, a process in three stages consisting of K.'s dialogue with the priest (*T*, 210–13), the Parable proper (*T*, 213–15), and its elucidation, in which K. joins the priest (*T*, 215–22). From its very inception, the Parable establishes an economy of endless interpretative supplantation and an ambiguity between exchange and delusion. It thus epitomizes, from the start, the literariness that the novel has set on display. "Don't be deluded," warns the priest, upon K.'s informing him that he is "an exception among those who belong to the Court," and noting that he has "more trust in you than any of the others" (*T*, 213). Yet the verb for "to delude," *täuschen*, is but an umlaut away from *tauschen*, "to exchange," appearing, among other places, in Leni's explanation of how she and K. have come to possess each other sexually. Implicit in this latter term is the priority of the movement of replacement spanning past and future encounters over any particular relation at hand. The novel's economy of literary exchange is only enriched by Kafka's carefully planted confusion of the economic and textual *tauschen* with the evaluative *täuschen*, the deception figuring so prominently in the novel's final theater of interpretation, the narration and exegesis of the Parable. *Tauschen* has insinuated itself into the novel at two conspicuous moments, when K. and Uncle Karl first spy Leni's eyes through the grille in Lawyer Huld's apartment door (*T*, 99), and just at the moment when she lures K. from his first legal consultation (*T*, 106). By the time the priest makes repeated use of *täuschen* to designate the Parable of the Doorkeeper as a whole and to characterize the misinterpretations to which it has given rise on the part of its characters and commentators, the play between almost identical verbs has long been established, so that in their multiplicity alone the various explanations offered by the priest also appear as deceptions: "In the writings which preface the Law that particular delusion (*Täuschung*) is described thus: before the Law stands a doorkeeper" (*T*, 213). "In this case there even exists an interpretation which claims that the deluded person (*der Getäuschte*) is really the doorkeeper" (*T*, 217). The play between *tauschen* and *täuschen* in the background of the Parable implies that the novel's successive explanations of the Law are its most authentic exchanges, but that these, like their verbal stem, are hardly to be distinguished from deceptions. The diverging interpretations entering this exchange implicate one another in a collective deceit.

If the Parable of the Doorkeeper provides no more authoritative commentary on the novel than appears in the story of K.'s confrontation with the Law, it is also characterized no less than the rest of the narrative by a relentless movement of hermeneutic supplantation. More important than the Parable's few thematic parallels with the story of K. is the prevalence of its movement of disqualification. In the light of this continuity, the canonical origin and imputed venerability setting the Parable in relief are to be viewed ironically. The setting off of the Parable from the remainder of the novel does, however, provide the reader with an opportunity to observe an isolated episode of this interpretative supplantation, one that must be acknowledged to be, however, neither more nor less privileged than any other instance of the replacement epitomizing the novel's textuality.

Certain details included in the narration and elucidation of the Parable do, of course, coincide with particularities of K.'s experience and to that extent serve a referential function. One can hardly avoid associating the "kleine Verhöre" ("brief conversation" [*T*, 213]) held between the doorkeeper and the man from the country with the hearings that are described and mentioned in the course of K.'s trial. It is also difficult to ignore the contrast between the doorkeeper's infinite patience (lapsing only when he wonders at the man's insatiable drive [*T*, 214]) and the impatience demonstrated by Block in imploring Huld to press his case (*T*, 177–78). But the most significant connection between the confrontation with the priest in the Cathedral and K.'s other encounters is the allegory of successive readers for which the entire novel serves as a setting. In the case of the exchange between K. and the priest, several levels of reading are spanned. K.'s initial reaction to the Parable is a naive understanding, deriving directly from the sequence of events. The doorkeeper is the deceiver and the man the victim because the doorkeeper never advises him of the futility of his efforts, yet refuses him entrance in the end. The priest's response to this formulation is a fuller and even self-contradictory commentary, at first presenting the doorkeeper in the best possible light as a civil servant, recognizing both the weight and the unimportance of his position, and then considering his potential flaws, evidence of his simplicity and arrogance in the narrative. Having captivated K. by the multiplicity of interpretations possibly attached to the doorkeeper, the priest is then free to transmit exegeses varying even more violently from K.'s literal reading. Thus, the man is really the master and the doorkeeper the slave, or the doorkeeper, as an instrument of the Law, is immune to human judgment. In the case of the Parable, then, an initially literal reading of the text is not so much negated as assimilated within an exegetical body permitting a wide, virtually unlimited variety of readings.

The allegory of reading in the Parable encompasses movements beyond the assimilation of naive and complex commentaries into one exegetical corpus. The man of the Parable is identified only as a "Mann vom Lande," a description suggesting a universal humanity of autochthonous origins as much as it does an unsophisticated person from the country. The story of the Parable describes the exclusion of this human being from the interior of the Law. The inclusiveness of the priest's readings fulfills the very freedom that the man has expended an entire lifetime to bring about. But the inclusion for which the man strives, like the trapeze artist's yearning to suspend his suspension, is a function of textuality, in this case, the textual quality of the

Law. The human yearning arises from the logical and rhetorical liberties taken by the text, from which, ironically, the human is categorically excluded. It is not accidental, then, that in his correction of K.'s primitive reading of the Parable, the priest should twice invoke the text's contradiction-suspending and duplicity-sustaining freedom:

> "The story contains two important statements made by the doorkeeper about admission to the Law, one at the beginning, the other at the end. The first statement is: that he cannot admit the man at the moment, and the other is: that this door was intended only for the man. If there were a contradiction between the two, you would be right and the doorkeeper would have deceived the man. But there is no contradiction. The first statement, on the contrary, even implies the second." (*T*, 215)

In this passage, the mutually negating conditions that can be apprehended by the human being only as a paradox not only fail to contradict, but are joined by implication. Complexity and variation are also what the priest brings to K.'s initially flat characterization of the doorkeeper. "The commentators note in this connection: 'The right perception of any matter and a misunderstanding of the same matter do not wholly exclude each other.' One must at any rate assume that such simpleness and conceit, however sparingly manifest, are likely to weaken his defense of the door; they are breaches (*Lücken*) in the character of the doorkeeper" (*T*, 216). The doorkeeper, in this internalized recapitulation of the novel's framework, is as susceptible to petty vanity as K. It is precisely at the point of the exegetical multiplicity accommodated by the priest as an instrument of the Law that the boundary between the human and the textual is demarcated. The priest is trying to inform K. of this limit when, as a rigorous explicator, he insists that he limit his interpretation of the Parable to what is inscribed in the text: " 'You have not enough respect for the written word and you are altering the story,' said the priest" (*T*, 215). Despite its internal accommodation of an unlimited set of variant readings, the domain of the Law is bounded by an absolute barrier proscribing the penetration of the textual by the existential. The most striking suggestion of this impenetrability comes in the priest's intimation that even the doorkeeper will succumb to human blindness and be excluded from the Law (*T*, 217–19). The doorkeeper is only to the "Mann vom Lande" what Lawyer Huld, Titorelli, Block, and the priest are to K.: textual mediators.[3] Their fate, even the priest's, is implied by the door-keeper's prospects. The Law has space only for its readings, not for its readers or most devoted servants. The end of the allegory of successive readers set in relief by the Parable of the Doorkeeper is that the inter-preters are all expendable, although interpretation is the nature of the Law. K. can at least appreciate this supplantation as the priest sends him off to death.

The Parable of the Doorkeeper may not hold water as a legal document, but it issues from the Holy of Holies, the inner court of lit-erary sensibility and design. Its literariness, however, is matched by the accuracy and ineluctability of its psychological laws. The fullest mea-sure of the Parable's uncanny instinct is its specification, "No one but you could gain admittance through this door, since this door was intended for you" (*T*, 214–15). To try to define the trial of language and consciousness with precision is ultimately as futile a task as it is for the "Mann vom Lande" to try to gain entry to the Law. Yet however the human child experiences the torment of awareness, whether as thwarted desire or familial nonempathy, or social isolation, or self-alienation, or as philosophical difference or indifference, the burden of interpretation, of reestablishing contact between the fragmentary drafts of apprehension and understanding, falls on him or her, alone or in meaningful commiseration with other human beings. The great irony of the novel and of the lives modeled on its particular insights and delusions, as the tradition of psychoanalysis has not failed to note, is that K., like the exemplary man of the Parable, could have walked out on "the meaningless affair" (*CS*, 432) at any time.

To undergo the trial, whether experienced as a curse or a mar-tyrdom, is to accept its conditions, to take responsibility for its bless-ings and curses, its rewards and punishments. The great irony of the novel is that we may not know exactly what the trial is, just as science and culture have not yet arrived at any definitive understandings of the self or consciousness, but that Joseph K. could have departed at any time from its elation and its torment, by critically examining its terms. That analysis might not have been a brief or easy one, but it was within his reach, as it would be within the reach of any contemplative person. In its cryptic inconclusiveness, Kafka's great fable of writing and life demonstrates that the way into the trial is the way out of it; the dynamics of the disease are the mechanism of its cure; and the unresolvable riddles of death, love, and language are its only keys.

Does the Parable of the Doorkeeper deepen K.'s and the reader's understanding, or does it comprise one final put-down? On this point the novel is hopelessly (or maliciously, as the case may be) unclear. No sooner has one exited from the precinct of the integrating Parable than its lesson sinks into murkiness. "The simple story had lost its clear outline, he wanted to put it out of his mind, and the priest, who now showed great delicacy of feeling, suffered him to do so and accepted his comment in silence, although undoubtedly he did not agree with it" (*T*, 221). The narration and discussion of the Parable had indeed ended on a controversial note. To the priest's injunction to accept the necessity of existing circumstances regardless of their truth value, K. had responded reproachfully, "It turns lying into a universal principle" (*T*, 220). More important than the outcome of this dispute are the rhythm and prospects for interpretation that it establishes, an alternation between insight and delusion, falling in and out of "the right perception of any matter" (*T*, 216). Not only K. but the clarity of parabolic understanding must succumb to the limit of the Law. Yet it is upon the question of the end result of the parable's insight that our understanding of the novel's equally self-referential and enigmatic "End" hinges.

"The End" is both a whirlwind reprise of the novel's sexual motif and the narration of a painful, embarrassing, and shameful execution. As I pointed out in chapter 7, Fräulein Bürstner or someone very much like her makes a return appearance on a stairway in a side street. At the same time, K.'s final arrest and conversation with his executioners was prophetic of the tactics characterizing the totalitarian regimes that held sway in major European nations throughout much of our century. The scene also belongs to the theater of the absurd, which it also heralded. And there is even some small hint in it that it comprises a turning point at which K. takes his fate into his own hands and achieves a dispassionate overview of his captors' and his own positions. It is in keeping with a novel hinging on the Parable of the Doorkeeper that its ending is complex, multiple, and ultimately inconclusive.

What propels the scene forward is the image of three men moving forward, with minor faux pas and interruptions, in lockstep, stepping to the ineluctable rhythm of time if not necessity. Implicit in this uniformity are both horrible repression, all the more dreadful for its nonspecificity, and some possibility for empathy or compassion (German: *Mitleid*).

Kafka's fictive art is above all one of configuration and dissolution; of drawing prior thematic and symbolic strands of the text together in order to release them to form new, even more radical constellations. Kafka generates meaning through the tightening of the threads of which texts are inevitably made. The final passage of *The Trial* comprises "files" we have been pursuing since its first chapter: references to and demonstrations of theatricality; K.'s alternation between estrangement and harmony with his cohorts; exaggerated formalities and the inevitable resistance to which they give rise; finding a pathway through a labyrinthine city and passing beyond it to a "killing field." Out of these already familiar materials Kafka fashions an ending worthy of *The Trial,* for all its inconclusiveness.

The two primary elements that give this conclusion any coherence it has to offer are the transformation of K.'s easily understood resistance to his captors into an uncannily placid harmony with them, and the equally unsettling juxtaposition (akin to the connections that poetic metaphors and psychological condensations make all the time) between the violence of K.'s execution and the utter politeness with which it is carried out.

As we might expect in a final, terminal reprise of the novel's major issues, K. responds initially to the henchmen with contempt, reinvoking the novel's overall aura of disbelief in the artificiality of its own events: " 'Tenth rate actors they send for me,' said K. to himself, glancing round again to confirm the impressions. 'They want to finish me off cheaply.' He turned abruptly toward the men and asked: 'What theater are you playing at?'" (*T*, 224). The narrative here again draws attention to its own theatricality; it records the transformation of K.'s "private" skepticism into a speech act of utter disbelief. The narrative voice "willingly" joins in a chorus of K.'s anger. " 'Perhaps they are tenors,' he thought as he studied their fat double chins. He was repelled by the painful cleanliness of their faces" (*T*, 224), by their well-tended, manicured look.

The cameo appearance of Fräulein Bürstner (or her simulacrum) in the scene becomes the watershed between K.'s resistance and his acquiescence to the horrible circumstances about to follow. This subepisode corresponds to a long, loving, but hopeless glance back to a disappearing life that, as I observed in chapter 7, the Kafkan protagonist makes as he succumbs to (or faces) his martyrdom. After Fräulein Bürstner disappears into a side street,

> K. could do without her and submitted himself to the guidance of his escort. In complete harmony all three now made their way across a bridge in the moonlight, the two men readily yielded to K.'s slightest movement, and when he turned slightly toward the parapet they turned, too, in a solid front. The water, glittering and trembling in the moonlight, divided on either side of a small island, on which the foliage of trees and buses rose in thick masses, as if bunched together. Beneath the trees ran gravel paths, now invisible, with convenient benches on which K. had stretched himself at ease many a summer. "I didn't mean to stop," he said to his companions, shamed by their obliging compliance. Behind K.'s back the one seemed to reproach the other gently for the mistaken stop they had made, and then all three went on again. (*T*, 226)

What is most striking in this passage is the harmony achieved by K. and his executioners, a glittering surface that belies the turmoil underneath it. Here, at the end of *The Trial,* Kafka returns to a setting, the scene of a crime, that he had elaborated in perhaps the first full demonstration of his fictive genius, the 1905 "Description of a Struggle." In this final scene of *The Trial* as in the earlier work, Kafka has his characters enter a labyrinthine landscape whose only organizing principle is the branchings and turnings that literary plots and associations achieve. It is in a quite conspicuously literary landscape that "the two men readily yielded to K.'s slightest movement," that all three "in complete harmony . . . in a solid front" pass divided and trembling waters, involuted foliage, and branching gravel paths. (Of subsequent twentieth-century writers, the Argentinian author and librarian Jorge Luis Borges will exploit the settings of fictive branching, bifurcation, and permutation to fullest advantage.)[4] The "glittering and trembling" surface of the water recalls visual imagery that the German romantic author and thinker Friedrich Schlegel associated with the literary mode of irony.[5]

Of all phenomena over which we could pause, it is K.'s bizarre, trembling peace with his captors, a surface of theatrical politeness and cooperation applied to the quaking depths of rage and terror, that strike us as the novel faces its own death, or at least its conclusion. One framework for this enigma that we have explored is the exhausting sequence of contempt, shame, and guilt within which K.'s "emotional life" is trapped. Are K.'s rage and guilt so painful, the scene asks us, that he could "feel" a certain relief, even at his own execution, even with the men who will stab him to death, having implicitly asked him to do their own dirty work for them? The narrative at least asks us to consider this possibility.

In my discussion of *The Trial,* I have paused carefully over what it means for K. to be the son of his society and of his environment, and what it means for his legacy to encompass the mark of art, if not of Cain. The novel's final scene directs our attention toward the third point of the triangle or trinity on which my interpretation has been structured. What is the nature of K.'s suffering and martyrdom? Is it the exquisitely painful consciousness of the oversensitive, underappreciated son? Does it take place with such a playful defiance that the scenario of martyrdom cannot be applied to it?

The execution has been scheduled for the nighttime of dreams and concealment. It takes place in "a small stone quarry, deserted and desolate" yet "quite near . . . a still completely urban house" (*T,* 227). The punitive act for a crime that has never been specified, that occurred, if anywhere, on the symbolic level, although its social, psychological, and moral grounds have been suggested, takes place in the kind of quarry ordinary gravestones might well come from, in a site very much within the pale of modern normality. (For all the uncanniness of the Court and its procedures and atmosphere, Kafka has avoided a "fantastic" ending for the novel.) "The moon shown down on everything with that simplicity and serenity which no other light possesses" (*T*, 227). This unremittingly clear illumination is not the moonlight of sorcery or madness but the lighting for a most fundamental and human drama. By the time the scene has ended K. will be reduced to a corpse, but the trial of his sensibility and its interpersonal implications will continue.

K. "dies" amid a flurry of gestures, a pantomime whose meaning is at once self-evident, absurd, and nonexistent.

> After an exchange of courteous formalities regarding which of them was to take precedence in the next task . . . one of them came up to K. and removed his coat, his waistcoat, and finally his shirt. K. shivered involuntarily, whereupon the man gave him a light, reassuring pat on the back. . . . The two of them laid K. down on the ground, propped him against the boulder, and settled his head upon it. But in spite of the pains they took and all the willingness K. showed, his posture remained contorted and unnatural-looking. . . . Then one of them opened his frock coat and out of a sheath that hung from a belt gird round his waistcoat drew a long, thin, double-edged butcher's knife, held it up, and tested the cutting edges in the moonlight. Once more the odious courtesies began, the first handed the knife across K. to the second, who handed it across K. back again to the first. K. now perceived clearly that he was supposed to seize the knife himself, as it traveled from hand to hand above him, and plunge it into his own breast. (*T*, 227–28)

Even K.'s death is party to a crisis in the mechanism and meaning of language. Amid "odious courtesies" the Court relieves K. a second time of his clothes. His executioners are oblivious to him as they pass back and forth the weapon for his murder, just as Hermann and Julie Kafka, by Franz Kafka's own account, spoke of him in the third person in his presence. The Court places him in a position possibly worse than the one in which his posture, messiah-like, "remained contorted and unnatural-looking." K. dies exposed. Perhaps the denuding of the body, the removal of the clothes that, within a civilized environment, mask the cycle of his rage and art, constitutes the shame that he expresses in his final words. Within the scene's implicit but incomprehensible sign language, the butcher's knife is a symbol with a long history in Kafka's work and thought. In "A Crossbreed" it is the instrument that would release the narrator from his anguish and his legacy, that would "do the thing of which both of us are thinking" (*CS,* 427). Its close "relative" is the ax in "A Country Doctor," the one that the aging doctor tells his congenitally wounded boy patient would "do" his wound "in a tight corner with two strokes of the ax" (*CS,* 225). With the hopelessness of the children and legacies in Kafka's fiction that cannot "do the thing of which [the executioners] are thinking," K. awaits the outcome of his trial.

> His glance fell on the top story of the house adjoining the quarry.
> . . . The casements of a window there suddenly flew open; a human figure, faint and insubstantial at that distance and that height, leaned abruptly far forward and stretched both arms still farther. Who was it? A friend? A good man? Someone who sympathized? Someone who wanted to help? Was it one person only? Or was it mankind? Was help at hand? Were there arguments in his favor that had been overlooked? Of course there must be. . . .
> But the hands of one of the partners were already at K.'s throat, while the other thrust the knife deep into his heart and turned it there twice. With failing eyes K. could still see the two of them immediately before him, cheek leaning against cheek, watching the final act. "Like a dog!" he said; it was as if the shame of it must outlive him. (*T,* 228–29)

So ends one of the most compelling explorations into the nature of the human mind and into the linguistic dynamics of the artifacts it fashions in the history of any literature. As if to underscore the sense of loss and separation aroused when K. catches a glimpse of "Fräulein Bürstner," the scene briefly cuts, cinematographically, to "a human figure, faint and insubstantial" outlined against a window. This is not a specific character but a generic human being, as universal as a "Mann vom Lande" who never penetrates the broader mysteries of his or her life. This basic human being, its human nature, like "the Judge whom he [K.] had never seen," like "the high Court to which he had never penetrated" (*T*, 228), is unknowable. K. is excluded from this knowledge, as the "Mann vom Lande" is withheld from the domain of the Law, as K. in his final moment is separated from the "human figure" by distance and a window frame. K. "dies" overwhelmed by the separation and difference that configure human thought, language, and art. He is a martyr, not of his life and times, but of the text. He succumbs in "pain" and "horror," leaving us the option of contemplating, in philosophical, psychological, and aesthetic terms, the meaning of the enigma, "No one but you could gain admittance through this door, since this door was intended for you" (*T*, 214–15).

K.'s shame will indeed outlive him, for it is the emotive correlative to insight. K.'s shame is the anguish of rigorously interpreting a world indifferent to his sensibility. K. "dies" at the end of the novel, as Franz Kafka succumbed to tubercular pneumonia, on 3 June 1924. Yet "The End" is rigorous in inscribing K.'s defiance, in noting that, after relinquishing his role as victim, he "forcibly pulled his companions forward" (*T*, 226). He even camouflages his execution to the police (*T*, 226–27), just as he once invoked the howl of a dog to "cover" the whipping scene in the bank. *The Trial* may pursue K.'s oppression and emotional roller coaster to a shameful and ignominious end, but with protracted defiance and generosity it suggests, as few artworks have managed, literature's resources as well: the irony, humor, proliferation, condensation, and distortion pointing the way beyond the door.

Notes and References

1. The History of an Image

1. Walter Benjamin, "The Image of Proust," *Illuminations,* ed. Hannah Arendt (New York: Schocken, 1969), 201.

2. Ronald Hayman, *Kafka: A Biography* (New York: Oxford University Press, 1981), xv, 183–84.

3. Carl E. Schorske, *Fin-de-siècle Vienna: Politics and Culture* (New York: Vintage, 1981).

4. "The Aeroplanes in Brescia," a report on Italy's first international "Flight Meeting," held 5–13 September 1909, published in the Prague daily, *Bohemia.*

5. Klaus Wagenbach, *Franz Kafka: Pictures of a Life,* trans. Arthur S. Wensinger (New York: Pantheon, 1984).

2. At the Crossroads of the Twentieth Century

1. *The Trial,* Definitive Edition (New York: Schocken Books, 1974); hereafter cited in text as *T.*

2. Henry Sussman, *Franz Kafka: Geometrician of Metaphor* (Madison: Coda Press, 1979), 158–59.

3. *Letter to His Father,* trans. Ernst Kaiser and Eithne Wilkins (New York: Schocken, 1971).

4. *The Complete Stories,* ed. Nahum S. Glatzer (New York: Schocken, 1976), 9–51, hereafter cited in text as *CS.*

5. Walter Benjamin, "Franz Kafka: On the Tenth Anniversary of His Death," *Illuminations,* 122; hereafter cited in text.

3. The Trial of Interpretation and Its Critical Reception

1. Sigmund Freud, *The Interpretation of Dreams,* in *The Standard Edition of the Complete Psychological Works of Sigmund Freud,* ed. J.

151

Stachey (London: Hogarth Press, 1953–74, 5: 506–8; hereafter cited in text.

2. See, for example, Larysa Mykyta, "Woman as the Obstacle and the Way," in *Critical Essays on Franz Kafka,* ed. Ruth V. Gross (Boston: G. K. Hall, 1990), 73–84.

3. Heinz Politzer, *Franz Kafka: Parable and Paradox* (Ithaca: Cornell University Press, 1962).

4. Walter Sokel, *Franz Kafka: Tragik und Ironie* (Munich, Germany: Albert Langen, 1964).

5. Wilhelm Emrich, *Franz Kafka: A Critical Study of His Writings,* trans. Sheema Zeben Buehne (New York: Frederick Ungar, 1968).

6. Edmund Wilson, "A Dissenting Opinion of Kafka," in *Kafka: A Collection of Critical Essays,* ed. Ronald Gray, (Englewood Cliffs, N.J.: Prentice-Hall, 1962), 91–98.

7. Maurice Blanchot, *The Space of Literature,* trans. Ann Smock (Lincoln: University of Nebraska Press, 1982).

8. Theodor Adorno, "Notes on Kafka," in *Prisms,* trans. Samuel Weber and Shierry Weber (Cambridge: MIT Press, 1984), 243–71.

9. James Rolleston, *Kafka's Narrative Theater* (University Park: Pennsylvania State University Press, 1974), xv.

10. Ronald Gray, *Franz Kafka* (Cambridge: Cambridge University Press, 1973).

11. Anthony Thorlby, *Kafka: A Study* (London: Heinemann, 1972).

12. Günther Anders, *Franz Kafka,* trans. A. Steer and A. K. Thorlby (London: Bowes and Bowes, 1960).

13. Walter Sokel, *Franz Kafka* (New York: Columbia University Press, 1966).

14. Walter Sokel, "The Programme of K.'s Court: Oedipal and Existential Meanings of *The Trial,*" in *On Kafka: Semi-Centenary Perspectives,* ed. Franz Kuna (London: Paul Elek, 1976), 1–21.

15. Marthe Robert, *Franz Kafka's Loneliness,* trans. Ralph Manheim (London: Faber and Faber, 1982).

16. Calvin S. Hall and Richard E. Lind, *Dreams, Life, and Literature: A Study of Franz Kafka* (Chapel Hill: University of North Carolina Press, 1970).

17. Heinz Kohut, *The Restoration of the Self* (Madison, Conn.: International Universities Press, 1977), 287–88.

18. Gilles Deleuze and Félix Guattari, *Kafka: Toward a Minor Literature* (Minneapolis: University of Minnesota Press, 1986).

19. Mark Spilka, *Dickens and Kafka: A Mutual Interpretation* (Bloomington: Indiana University Press, 1963).

Notes and References

20. Franz Kuna, *Kafka: Literature as Corrective Punishment* (Bloomington: Indiana University Press, 1974).

21. Michel Foucault, *Discipline and Punish,* trans. Alan Sheridan (New York: Pantheon Books, 1977).

22. Jack Murray, *Landscapes of Alienation: Ideological Deconstruction in Kafka, Céline, and Onetti* (Stanford: Stanford University Press, 1991).

23. Robert Rochefort, *Kafka, où L'Irréductible espoir* (Paris: René Julliard, 1947).

24. Paul Goodman, *Kafka's Prayer* (New York: Vanguard Press, 1947).

25. Charles Neider, *The Frozen Sea* (New York: Oxford University Press, 1948).

26. Martin Greenberg, *The Terror of Art: Kafka and Modern Literature* (New York: Basic Books, 1968).

27. Michel Carrouges, *Kafka versus Kafka,* trans. Emmet Parker (Tuscaloosa: University of Alabama Press, 1968).

28. Jill Robbins, *Prodigal Son/Elder Brother: Interpretation and Alterity in Augustine, Petrarch, Kafka, and Levinas* (Chicago: University of Chicago Press, 1991).

29. Stanley Corngold, *The Commentator's Despair: The Interpretation of Kafka's "Metamorphosis"* (Port Washington, N.Y.: Kennicat Press, 1973).

30. Henry Sussman, "The Court as Text: Inversion, Supplanting, and Derangement in Kafka's *Der Prozeß*," *PMLA* 92 (1977): 41–55.

31. Henry Sussman, *Franz Kafka: Geometrician of Metaphor* (Madison: Coda Press, 1979).

32. Alan Udoff, ed., *Kafka and the Contemporary Critical Performance* (Bloomington: Indiana University Press, 1987).

33. Charles Bernheimer, *Kafka and Flaubert* (New Haven: Yale University Press, 1982).

34. Hans Helmut Hiebel, *Die Zeichen des Gestezes: Recht und Macht bei Franz Kafka* (Munich, Germany: Wilhelm Fink Verlag, 1983).

35. Stanley Corngold, *Franz Kafka: The Necessity of Form* (Ithaca: Cornell University Press, 1988).

36. Clayton Koelb, *Kafka's Rhetoric: The Passion of Reading* (Ithaca: Cornell University Press, 1988).

37. Henry Sussman, *Afterimages of Modernity: Structure and Indifference in Twentieth-Century Literature* (Baltimore: Johns Hopkins University Press, 1990).

38. Jean-Michel Rey, *Quelqu'un danse: Les Noms de F. Kafka* (Lille, France: Presses Universitaires de Lille, 1985).

39. Malcolm Pasley and Ulrich Ott, *Franz Kafka, "Der Prozeß": Die Handschrift Redet,* in *Marbacher Magazin* 52 (1990).

40. Max Brod, *Franz Kafka: A Biography,* trans. G. Humphreys Roberts and Richard Winston (New York: Schocken Books, 1960).

41. Gustav Janouch, *Conversations with Kafka,* trans. Goronwy Rees (London: Quartet Books, 1985).

42. Klaus Wagenbach, *Franz Kafka: Eine Biographie seiner Jugend* (Bern, Switzerland: Franke, 1958).

43. Elias Canetti, *Kafka's Other Trial: The Letters to Felice,* trans. Christopher Middleton (London: Calder and Boyars, 1974).

44. Pietro Citati, *Kafka,* trans. Raymond Rosenthal (New York: Alfred A. Knopf, 1990).

45. Harold Bloom, ed., *Franz Kafka's "The Trial,"* Modern Critical Interpretations (New York: Chelsea House, 1987).

46. Angel Flores, ed., *The Kafka Problem* (New York: Octagon Books, 1963).

47. Ronald Gray, ed., *Kafka,* Twentieth Century Views (Englewood Cliffs, N.J.: Prentice-Hall, 1962).

48. Kenneth Hughes, ed., *Franz Kafka: An Anthology of Marxist Criticism* (Hanover, N.H.: University Press of New England, 1981).

49. Franz Kuna, ed., *On Kafka: Semi-Centenary Perspectives* (London: Paul Elek, 1976).

50. James Rolleston, ed., *Twentieth-Century Interpretations of "The Trial"* (Englewood Cliffs, N.J.: Prentice-Hall, 1976).

51. J. P. Stern, ed., *The World of Franz Kafka* (London: Weidenfeld and Nicolson, 1980).

52. Ruth V. Gross, *Critical Essays on Franz Kafka* (Boston: G. K. Hall, 1990).

4. Rehearsals

1. Joachim Unseld provides an illuminating publication history of Kafka's works, one by one, in *Franz Kafka: Ein Schriftstellerleben* (Munich, Germany: Carl Hanser Verlag, 1982), from which my information on the early appearances of the short fiction and *The Trial* is taken.

2. Twentieth-century social sciences and critical theory have undertaken a rather full exploration of the gift as a social phenomenon and the conceptual and affective ambivalence attending it. Among the highpoints of this inquiry are Marcel Mauss's groundbreaking study, *The Gift: Forms and Functions of Exchange in Archaic Societies,* trans. Ian Cunnison (New York: W. W. Norton, 1967) and Georges Bataille's elaborations on potlatch and sacrifice, in such

essays as "The Notion of Expenditure" and "Sacrifices," in his *Visions of Excess: Selected Writings, 1927–39,* ed. Allan Stoekl (Minneapolis: University of Minnesota Press), 116–36. Also crucial in this regard is Jacques Derrida's teasing out of the gift dimension (as poison and present) in the Platonic *pharmakon,* itself an emblem for Western culture's volatile attitude toward the notation, contingency, and play that Derrida terms *writing.* See "Plato's Pharmacy," in *Dissemination,* trans. Barbara Johnson (Chicago: University of Chicago Press, 1981), 128–33.

3. Among several possible examples, see, in this regard, "Memoires of the Kalda Railroad," in *The Diaries of Franz Kafka: 1914–1923,* ed. Max Brod (New York: Schocken, 1965), 79–91.

4. See Henry Sussman, "An American History Lesson: Hegel and the Historiography of Superimposition," in *Theorizing American History,* ed. Bainard Cowan and Joseph Kronick (Baton Rouge: Louisiana State University Press, 1991), 33–52.

5. A Courthouse of Codes and Messages

1. Roland Barthes, *S/Z: An Essay,* trans. Richard Miller (New York: Hill and Wang, 1986), 3–6, 18–35.

2. James Rolleston, *Kafka's Narrative Theater* (University Park: Pennsylvania State University Press, 1974), xv–xvi, 69–87.

3. See Sigmund Freud, "Studies on Hysteria," in the *Standard Edition,* 2: 11–12, 23–24, 33–34, 37–47, 123–24, 133–34, 220–21, 225–31, 233–39, and 249–50.

4. Immanuel Kant, *Critique of Pure Reason,* trans. Norman Kemp Smith (New York: St. Martin's Press, 1965), 298–300.

5. I think here of the Freudian patients known as Dora, Little Hans, the Rat Man, Daniel Paul Schreber, and the Wolf Man, whose case histories, respectively, have been published in the *Standard Edition* under the following titles: "A Case of Hysteria" (7:15–122); "Analysis of a Phobia in a Five-Year-Old Boy" (10:5–149); "Notes upon a Case of Obsessional Neurosis" (10:153–318); "Psycho-Analytical Notes on an Autobiographical Account of a Case of Paranoia (Dementia Paranoides)" (12:3–82); and "From the History of an Infantile Neurosis" (17:3–121).

6. Bearings

1. Fyodor Dostoyevski's *Crime and Punishment* may well be the most influential single literary "source" for *The Trial.* Not only do the crowded and oppressive police offices in Dostoyevski's novel prefigure similar bureaucratic spaces in *The Trial* and *The Castle,* but Kafka extends the impoverished realism of Raskolnikov's neighborhood into the urban settings where K.'s prelim-

inary hearing and Titorelli's apartment are located. In a Kafkan manner, Dostoyevski compresses virtually all the major characters in *Crime and Punishment* into two or three apartments in Raskolnikov's neighborhood. Kafka's spatial humor was most receptive to characters such as false-murderer Nikolay who, late in Dostoyevski's novel, appear (as Block does) out of nowhere from behind partitions, where they have been hiding for an indeterminate time. Conceptually, Dostoyevski's most substantial contribution to *The Trial* is the cat-and-mouse game between Raskolnikov and examining magistrate Porphyry. The latter character, in his dissimulation and irony, is worthy of the Kafkan Law in its elusiveness. For a sequence of passages indicating Dostoyevski's prefiguration of Kafka's spatial imagination, see Fyodor Dostoyevski, *Crime and Punishment,* trans. David Magarshack (New York: Penguin Books, 1951), 105, 113, 330–32, 346–49, 365–68, 449, 458, 472–73.

2. See Kafka's "Description of a Struggle," in which the overweight Fat Man addresses the following questions to the scrawny Supplicant (a Franz Kafka look-alike): "I guessed from the very beginning the state you are in. Isn't it something like a fever, a seasickness on land, a kind of leprosy?" (*CS,* 33).

3. See Sigmund Freud, *The Interpretation of Dreams, Standard Edition* 4: 24, 37–38, 202, 238–40, 247, 271–73, 285–89, 305, 326; 5: 355, 364–66, 369–72, 384, 392–95, 590, 684.

4. Roland Barthes, *A Lover's Discourse,* trans. Richard Howard (New York: Hill and Wang, 1984), 1, 3–9, 20–21, 28, 85, 132–33, 147–54.

5. On the notion of transgression, see Georges Bataille, "Histoire de l'érotisme," in *Oeuvres complètes* (Paris: Gallimard, 1970), 7:7–25.

7. The Society of Withdrawal

1. The American psychoanalyst Heinz Kohut is quite suggestive on the emotion of shame and its psychological and interpersonal contexts; see his *The Analysis of the Self* (Madison, Conn., International Universities Press, 1971), 181, 184.

2. Sigmund Freud, "Studies on Hysteria." Also see "The 'Uncanny,' " *Standard Edition,* 17:217–52.

3. See Joseph Conrad, *Lord Jim,* ed. Morton Dauwen Zabel (Boston: Houghton Mifflin, 1958), 33, 58, 69, 161, 233, 237, 260, 300.

8. The Parable of Parables

1. For the notion of psychoanalysis as a confrontation between grandiose and up-to-date drafts or versions of the self, see Kohut, *The Analysis of the Self,* 13–14, 26–27, 94–98, 143–45, 178, 210–12.

Notes and References

2. Textual mediators are so crucial to Heinz Politzer's conception of the operation of Kafka's novels that he devotes three separate sections of his *Franz Kafka: Parable and Paradox* to these "Information Givers"; see 148–50, 200–11, 252–62. Also see Beda Allemann, "Franz Kafka: *Der Prozeß*," in *Der Deutsche Roman,* ed. Benno von Wiese (Dusseldorf, Germany: Bagel, 1965), 2:268–72.

3. See Jorge Luis Borges, *Ficciones,* ed. Anthony Kerrigan (New York: Grove Press, 1962), 28, 75–76, 93, 96, 98. Also see Henry Sussman, "Kafka in the Heart of the Twentieth Century: An Approach to Borges," in *Afterimages of Modernity,* 156–60.

4. Friedrich Schlegel, *Friedrich Schlegel's Lucinde and the Fragments,* trans. Peter Firchow (Minneapolis: University of Minnesota Press, 1971), 154–55, 175–77, 195, 205–06, 234–36.

Bibliography

Primary Sources

The Complete Stories. Edited by Nahum N. Glatzer. New York: Schocken Books, 1976.

Diaries 1914–1923. Edited by Max Brod. New York: Schocken Books, 1965.

Definitive Edition. *The Trial.* Translated by Willa Muir and Edwin Muir. New York: Schocken Books, 1974.

Secondary Sources

Adorno, Theodor W. "Notes on Kafka." In *Prisms,* translated by Samuel Weber and Shierry Weber, 243–71. Cambridge: MIT Press, 1984. A Frankfurt school reading, much in the style of Benjamin's (see below).

Allemann, Beda. "Franz Kafka: *Der Prozeß.*" In *Der Deutsche Roman,* vol. 2, edited by Benno von Wiese. Dusseldorf, Germany: Bagel, 1965. Fine general reading, within a broad historical perspective.

Anders, Günther. *Franz Kafka.* Translated by A. Steer and A. K. Thorlby. London: Bowes and Bowes, 1960.

Barthes, Roland. *S/Z.* Translated by Richard Howard. New York: Hill and Wang, 1974. This is a demonstration of Barthesian semiology in action, specifically, as applied to "Sarrazine," a sexually ambiguous tale by Balzac. Barthes's division of the text into its semiological codes provided a methodological model for my approach to *The Trial*.

Bataille, Georges. "Histoire de l'érotisme." In *Oeuvres complètes*, 7:7–25. Paris: Gallimard, 1970. This long essay, as well as "La part maudite," serves as a manifesto for Bataille's notion of the transgression common to desire and literary work.

Benjamin, Walter. "Franz Kafka: On the Tenth Anniversary of His Death" and "Some Reflections on Kafka." In *Illuminations*, edited by Hannah Arendt, 111–46. New York: Schocken Books, 1969. This is perhaps the greatest work of Kafka criticism ever written, for it dramatizes Kafka's relation to history, narration, and textuality at the same time that it analyzes it. Benjamin's "mosaic technique" is in bloom here. I have discussed this great essay at length in "The Herald: A Reading of Walter Benjamin's Kafka Study" in *Diacritics* 7 (1977), 42–54; and in *Franz Kafka: Geometrician of Metaphor* (Madison, Wis.: Coda Press, 1979).

Bernheimer, Charles. *Flaubert and Kafka*. New Haven: Yale University Press, 1982. Discusses Flaubert's "influence" on Kafka, but in a theoretically and historically exciting way, in terms of "psychopoetics."

Binder, Hartmut. *Motive und Gestaltung bei Franz Kafka*. Bonn, Germany: H. Bouvier, 1966. Here, as in the entry immediately following, Binder furnishes philosophically and linguistically solid exegeses of Kafka's individual works.

——. *Kafka in neuer Sicht*. Stuttgart, Germany: J. B. Metzler, 1976.

Blanchot, Maurice. *The Space of Literature*. Translated by Ann Smock. Lincoln: University of Nebraska Press, 1982. For Blanchot, who is perhaps France's most theoretically important "purely" literary critic, Kafka exemplifies literarity, in the appropriately involuted and complex spaces he fabulates, and in his explicit relationships to the body and death.

Brod, Max. *Franz Kafka: A Biography*. Translated by G. Humphreys Roberts and Richard Winston. New York: Schocken Books, 1960. For many years, the standard biography, written by Kafka's lifelong intimate friend and literary executor.

Canetti, Elias. *Kafka's Other Trial: The Letters to Felice*. Translated by Christopher Middleton. New York: Schocken Books, 1974. An in-depth view of Kafka's stormy relationship with his three-time fiancée, illustrative of his generally problematical associations with women.

Carrouges, Michel. *Kafka versus Kafka*. Translated by Emmett Parker. Tuscaloosa: University of Alabama Press, 1962. An early general literary introduction to the major works and interpersonal issues, above all marriage and Kafka's struggle with his father.

Citati, Pietro. *Kafka.* Translated by Raymond Rosenthal. New York: Alfred A. Knopf, 1990.

Corngold, Stanley. *The Commentators' Despair: The Interpretation of Kafka's "Metamorphosis."* Port Washington, N.Y.: Kennikat Press, 1973. Arising out of Corngold's close affiliation with Paul de Man, this interpretative allegory is an early indication of the depth critical theory will impart to Kafka studies.

——. *Franz Kafka: The Necessity of Form.* Ithaca: Cornell University Press, 1988. Collected contributions over the years by a major American Kafka critic and Germanist.

Deleuze, Gilles, and Félix Guattari. *Kafka: Toward a Minor Literature.* Minneapolis: University of Minnesota Press, 1986. This is a major contribution, suggesting the psychopolitical dimension of Kafka's work, a domain that has yet to be fully explored.

Emrich, Wilhelm. *Franz Kafka: A Critical Study of His Writings.* Translated by Sheema Zeben Buehne. New York: Frederick Ungar, 1968. A classic general study.

Flores, Angel, ed. *The Kafka Problem.* New York: Octagon, 1963. A precedent-setting anthology.

——, ed. *The Kafka Debate: New Perspectives for Our Time.* New York: Gordian Press, 1977.

Foucault, Michel. *Discipline and Punish.* Translated by Alan Sheridan. New York: Pantheon Books, 1977. A major theoretical meditation on the history and epistemology of penal thought and practice.

Foulkes, A. P. *The Reluctant Pessimist: A Study of Franz Kafka.* The Hague: Mouton, 1967. A theological contribution.

Freud, Sigmund. *Three Essays on the Theory of Sexuality.* In *The Standard Edition of the Complete Psychological Writings of Sigmund Freud,* edited by J. Strachey, 7: 123–243. London: Hogarth Press, 1953–74. This and the Freudian entries immediately following demonstrates the close affinity between the emerging Freudian corpus and Kafka's near-contemporary writing.

——. "A Note on the Unconscious in Psycho-Therapy." In *The Standard Edition,* 12:255–66.

——. "Repression." In *The Standard Edition,* 14:141–58.

——. "On Beginning the Treatment" ("Further Recommendations on the Techique of Psycho-Analysis"). In *The Standard Edition,* 12:121–44.

——. "The 'Uncanny.'" In *The Standard Edition,* 17:217–52.

Goodman, Paul. *Kafka's Prayer.* New York: Vanguard Press, 1947. An existential approach to Kafka's fiction. Subjects considered include knowledge, guilt, self-destruction, and "constructive will."

Bibliography

Gray, Richard T. *Constructive Destruction: Kafka's Aphorism: Literary Tradition and Literary Transformation.* Tübingen, Germany: Max Niemeyer, 1987. Discusses Kafka's fragmentary prose, in the context of the history of the aphorism, contemporary aphorists, and the theory of the fragment.

Gray, Ronald. *Franz Kafka.* Cambridge: Cambridge University Press, 1973. A fine introduction and elucidation.

Greenberg, Martin. *The Terror of Art: Kafka and Modern Literature.* New York: Basic Books, 1968. A broad placement of such works as *The Trial,* "The Judgment," and "The Metamorphosis" in the contexts of existentialism and theology.

Gross, Ruth V., ed. *Critical Essays on Franz Kafka.* Boston: G. K. Hall, 1990. Gross's introduction on the proliferation of and necessity for anthologies of Kafka criticism is indispensable: it furnishes a context for the considerable number of anthologies listed even in so brief a bibliography as this one.

Hall, Calvin S., and Richard E. Lind. *Dreams, Life, and Literature: A Study of Franz Kafka.* Chapel Hill: University of North Carolina Press, 1970. In parallel, content analyses of Kafka's dreams and works. An attempt, in the spirit of the psychoanalytical reader-response criticism of Norman Holland, to view Kafka's works and dreams in relation to his personality.

Hayman, Ronald. *Kafka: A Biography.* New York: Oxford University Press, 1981. Draws heavily on the writings in deducing the life. Titillating in its openness to the sexual possibilities.

Heller, Erich. "The World of Franz Kafka." In *The Disinherited Mind,* 197–231. New York: Meridian Books, 1959. A classic placement of Kafka within the tradition of German letters.

——. *Franz Kafka.* Modern Masters. New York: Viking Press, 1974.

Heller, Peter. "Kafka: The Futility of Striving." In *Dialectics and Nihilism,* 227–306. Amherst: University of Massachusetts Press, 1966.

Hiebel, Hans Helmut. *Die Zeichen des Gesetzes: Recht und Macht bei Franz Kafka.* Munich, Germany: Wilhelm Fink Verlag, 1983. An important consideration of the literary status of the Law by a critic considered by Richard Jayne and others to be the most important theoretical Kafka critic writing in German.

Hughes, Kenneth, ed. *Franz Kafka: An Anthology of Marxist Criticism.* Hanover, N.H.: University Press of New England, 1981. Excellent collection of Marxist perspectives.

Janouch, Gustav. *Conversations with Kafka.* Translated by Goronwy Rees. London: Quartet Books, 1985. Indispensable contemporary reminiscences of Kafka at work and in life.

Jayne, Richard. *Erkenntnis und Transzendenz: Zur Hermeneutik literarische Texte Kafka.* Munich, Germany: Wilhelm Fink, 1983. An early work by a critic who has continued to offer important theoretical insight into Kafka's writings.

Kaiser, Gerhard. "Franz Kafkas 'Prozeß': Versuch einer Interpretation." *Euphorion* 52 (1958): 38-49. An important, careful reading of *The Trial.*

Kobs, Jörgen. *Kafka: Untersuchungen zu Bewußtsein und Sprache seiner Gestalten.* Bad Homburg, Germany: Athenäum, 1970. Careful, intelligent work.

Koelb, Clayton. *Kafka's Rhetoric: The Passion of Reading.* Ithaca: Cornell University Press, 1989. One of the most important theoretical approaches of recent years.

Kohut, Heinz. *The Restoration of the Self.* Madison, Conn.: International Universities Press, 1977. Kohut is the post-Freudian, object-relations psychoanalytical theorist who has most fully explored the notion of the grandiose. This concept is a capital one for literary studies, since so many of the most memorable works, such as *The Trial,* involve characters themselves fluctuating between grandiosity (classically known as hubris) and a compensatory shame.

Kraft, Werner. *Franz Kafka.* Frankfurt, Germany: Suhrkamp Verlag, 1968. Kraft responded early and intelligently to Kafka, in brief essays sharing the compression of his subject's fiction.

Kuna, Franz. *Franz Kafka: Literature as Corrective Punishment.* Bloomington: Indiana University Press, 1974. This work pursues the motifs of crime and punishment in Kafka's major writings.

——. ed. *On Kafka: Semi-Centenary Perspectives.* London: Paul Elek, 1976.

Kurz, Gerhard. *Traum-Schrecken: Kafkas literarische Existenzanalyse.* Stuttgart, Germany: J. B. Metzler, 1980. Eschewing psychoanalytical interpretations, this work explores the implications of the Kafkan protagonists' experiences for Being and Self.

Marson, Eric. *Kafka's "Trial:" The Case against Josef K.* St. Lucia, Australia: University of Queensland Press, 1975. Examines Joseph K.'s trial both as a legal procedure and as a process of reading and interpretation.

Murray, Jack. *Landscapes of Alienation: Ideological Deconstruction in Kafka, Céline, and Onetti.* Stanford: Stanford University Press, 1991. An excellent ideological reading of Kafka's *Amerika* in terms of the same inhuman spatial environment that predominates in *The Trial.*

Neider, Charles. *The Frozen Sea.* New York: Oxford University Press, 1948. A good early review of the then-existing critical literature and issues, followed by readings of the short fiction and novels, limited only by the state of the psychoanalytical theory of its day.

Bibliography

Philippi, Klaus-Peter. *Reflexion und Wirklichkeit: Untersuchungen zu Kafkas Roman "Das Schloß."* Tübingen, Germany: Max Niemeyer, 1966. A careful, intelligent reading of the Kafkan novel shedding most light on *The Trial.*

Politzer, Heinz. *Franz Kafka: Parable and Paradox.* Ithaca: Cornell University Press, 1962. A classical general study, in terms of the personal and logical anomalies that Kafka explores.

Rey, Jean-Michel. *Quelqu'un danse: Les Noms de F. Kafka.* Lille, France: Presses Universitaires de Lille, 1985. A critical dance, in keeping with the title, touching on the most intriguing implications of naming, signification, and representation in Kafka's texts.

Robbins, Jill. *Prodigal Son/Elder Brother: Interpretation and Alterity in Augustine, Petrarch, Kafka, and Levinas.* Chicago: University of Chicago Press, 1991. Contains a hermeneutic reading of the parables in terms of the latest theory of this process.

Robert, Marthe. *Franz Kafka's Loneliness.* Translated by Ralph Manheim. London: Faber and Faber, 1982. A discussion of Kafka's work and life in terms of the multiple forms of repression he encountered.

Robertson, Ritchie. *Kafka: Judaism, Politics, and Literature.* Oxford: Clarendon Press, 1985. Discussions of different works, among them the novels, "The Judgment," and the aphorisms, in the contexts of Kafka's Judaism and his political concerns.

Rochefort, Robert. *Kafka, où L'Irréductible espoir.* Paris: René Julliard, 1947. One of the richest theological treatments, viewing Kafka's works in the contexts of the secularization of society and the disappearance of God. The hope hinted at by the title is ontotheological in nature.

Rolleston, James. *Kafka's Narrative Theater.* University Park: Pennsylvania State University Press, 1974. An important placement of Kafka's work in an overall context of literary theatricality.

——, ed. *Twentieth-Century Interpretations of "The Trial."* Englewood Cliffs, N.J.: Prentice-Hall, 1976.

Scholem, Gershom G. *Major Trends in Jewish Mysticism.* New York: Schocken Books, 1973. By familiarizing oneself with this classic introduction into the Kabbalah and its Zohar, one learns the sources of certain distinctly Kafkan phenomena, such as the endless panorama of gates to the Law in *The Trial* and the similar procession of bureaucratic barriers in *The Castle.*

Schorske, Carl E. *Fin-de-siècle Vienna: Politics and Culture.* New York: Vintage, 1981. Much of what Schorske has to say about Vienna, in terms of its political extremism, its shaky economy, and its cultural milieu, also applies to the Prague that served as a setting and inspiration for many of Kafka's works.

Sokel, Walter H. *Franz Kafka: Tragik und Ironie.* Munich, Germany: Albert Langen, 1964. Excellent general study in terms of rhetoric and literary genre.

—. "The Programme of K.'s Court: Oedipal and Existential Readings of *The Trial.*" In *On Kafka: Semi-Centenary Perspectives,* edited by Franz Kuna, 1–21. London: Paul Elek, 1976. A good literary application of the Oedipus complex to *The Trial.*

—. "The Three Endings of Josef K. and the Role of Art in *The Trial.*" In Angel Flores, ed., *The Kafka Debate: New Perspectives for Our Time,* 335–53. New York: Gordian Press, 1977.

Spann, Meno. *Franz Kafka.* World Authors Series. Boston: G. K. Hall, 1976. A fine general introduction.

Spilka, Mark. *Dickens and Kafka: A Mutual Interpretation.* Bloomington: Indiana University Press, 1963. A highly suggestive exercise in comparative literature as comparison. Others who have been treated in relation to Kafka in this way (or need to be) are Kleist, Flaubert, and Dostoyevski.

Stern, J. P., ed. *The World of Franz Kafka.* London: Weidenfeld and Nicolson, 1980.

Sussman, Henry. "The Court as Text: Inversion, Supplanting, and Derangement in Kafka's *Der Prozeß.*" *PMLA* 90 (1977): 41–55.

—. *Franz Kafka: Geometrician of Metaphor.* Madison, Wis.: Coda Press, 1979.

—. *Afterimages of Modernity: Structure and Indifference in Twentieth-Century Literature.* Baltimore: Johns Hopkins University Press, 1990.

Thorlby, Anthony. *Kafka: A Study.* London: Heinemann, 1972.

Tiefenbrun, Ruth. *A Moment of Torment: An Interpretation of Franz Kafka's Short Stories.* Carbondale: Southern Illinois University Press, 1973. A psychologically astute reading from the perspectives of sadomasochism and suffering.

Udoff, Alan, ed. *Kafka and the Contemporary Critical Performance.* Bloomington: Indiana University Press, 1987. A collection marked by the highest level of theoretical sophistication.

Unseld, Joachim. *Franz Kafka: Ein Schriftstellerleben.* Munich, Germany: Carl Hanser, 1982. An indispensable account of the fates undergone by Kafka's works, during his life and after.

Wagenbach, Klaus. *Franz Kafka: Eine Biographie seiner Jugend.* Bern, Switzerland: Franke, 1958. The first authoritative biographical account after Brod's.

—. *Franz Kafka: Pictures of a Life.* Translated by Arthur S. Wensinger. New York: Pantheon, 1984. A marvelous resource book whose photographic evidence chronicles developments and inventions that took place in Kafka's Prague and that visually brings to life the environment that Kafka inhabited.

West, Rebecca. *The Court and the Castle: Some Treatments of a Recurrent Theme.* New Haven: Yale University Press, 1957.

Index

Adorno, Theodor, 24, 152, 158
aesthetics, 15–16, 35–37, 40, 42, 45,
    54, 57, 60, 64, 76–77, 80, 85,
    96–97, 99, 111–112, 129–31,
    137–38, 150
Afterimages of Modernity. See
    Sussman, Henry
Alice in Wonderland. See Carroll,
    Lewis
alienation, 3, 27, 60, 86, 96–97,
    112–115, 118–21, 143
allegory, 19, 49, 54, 57, 68, 70, 89,
    127, 129–31, 141
Allemann, Beda, 157–58
ambivalence, 40, 59, 106–7, 131
Amerika. See Kafka, Franz
Analysis of the Self, The. See Kohut,
    Heinz
Anders, Günther, 25, 152, 158
antinomies. *See* paradoxes
aphorism, 56
Archduke Franz Ferdinand, 5
architecture, 11, 66, 71, 98–101,
    103, 124, 127–29

artist, the, 11, 13, 28, 35, 37, 40,
    43–45, 50–61, 76, 109, 112,
    119, 121, 123, 129

Balzac, Honoré de, 63; "Sarrazine,"
    63–64
Barthes, Roland, 29, 63–64, 104,
    155–56, 158–59; *S/Z,* 63, 155,
    158–59
Bataille, Georges, 5, 104, 154–56,
    159; *Histoire de l'érotisme,*
    104
Bauer, Felice, x–xi, 107
Beckett, Samuel, 5, 30
Benjamin, Walter, 3, 16, 22–24, 28,
    151, 159
Bernheimer, Charles, 29, 153, 159
Blanchot, Maurice, 5, 24, 152, 159;
    The Space of Literature, 24,
    152, 159
Bloom, Harold, 30, 154
borderline, the, 62
Borges, Jorge Luis, 5, 147, 157
Bosch, Hieronymus, 39

Brave New World. See Huxley, Aldous

Brod, Max, x, xii, 30, 154, 159

"Bucket Rider, The." *See* Kafka, Franz

"Burrow, The." *See* Kafka, Franz

Camus, Albert, 72, 88, 115; *The Stranger,* 115

Canetti, Elias, 30, 154, 159

"Cares of a Family Man, The." See Kafka, Franz

Carroll, Lewis, 73, 98; *Alice in Wonderland,* 73

Carrouges, Michel, 28, 153, 159

Castle, The. See Kafka, Franz

Céline, Louis–Ferdinand, 27

"Children on a Country Road." *See* Kafka, Franz

Citati, Petro, 30, 154, 160

clothing as costume, 70–71

comparative literature, 97

Complete Stories, The. See Kafka, Franz

condensation, 66, 70, 91, 99, 150

Conrad, Joseph, 135, 156

contempt, 16, 48, 52, 65, 79–80, 86, 92, 105, 113, 121, 145, 147

Corngold, Stanley, 29–30, 153, 160

costume, see clothing

"Country Doctor, A." *See* Kafka, Franz

Cranach, Lucas, 39

Crime and Punishment. See Dostoyevski, Fyodor

critical approaches to *The Trial,* 19–31; deconstructive, 20, 28–29; feminist, 21–22; "literary," 23–25; Marxist, 20; psychoanalytical, 21–22, 25–27; sociological, 20–21, 24, 27, 88; structuralist, 20, 29; theological, 27–28

Critique of Pure Reason, The. See Kant, Immanuel

"Crossbreed, A [A Sport]." *See* Kafka, Franz

deceive (*täuschen*), 102, 139–41

deconstruction, 17, 21, 27–29. *See also* critical approaches to *The Trial*

"definite acquittal," 126–27

deformity, physical, 13, 59, 69–70, 106, 128

Deleuze, Gilles, 27, 152, 160

depth psychology, 50, 113

derangement. *See* disorientation

Derrida, Jacques, 17, 29, 155

"Description of a Struggle." *See* Kafka, Franz

Diaries 1914–23. See Kafka, Franz

Discourse of the Accused, 94

Discourse of the Father, 48, 94

Discourse of the Law, 73, 94, 117–18

Discourse of the Son, 48

disfiguration, 5

disorientation, 11, 27, 65, 91, 100–102, 120, 122, 128, 132, 134, 146

displacement, 19, 102–103, 106, 108, 116–17, 124, 139–43, 146–47, 150

distraction, 115–16

Dostoyesvski, Fyodor, 72, 88, 100, 115, 155–56; *Crime and Punishment,* 72, 100, 155–56

doubling, 48–50, 54–56, 86, 98, 109–11, 141–43

Duchamp, Marcel, 44

Dymant, Dora, xii–xiii

ego psychology, 26

Eliot, T. S., 97

empathy, 15, 25, 145

Emrich, Wilhelm, 23, 29, 152, 160

Index

engagement, marital, 46–48, 107
exchange (*tauschen*), 102, 117, 134, 139–40
extension. *See* proliferation

fables. *See* parables
Fairbairn, W. R. D., 26
Faulkner, William, 4
Fin de Siècle Vienna: Politics and Culture. See Schorske, Carl E.
Finnegans Wake. See Joyce, James
"First Sorrow." *See* Kafka, Franz
Flores, Angel, 30, 154, 160
Foucault, Michel, 27, 29, 153, 160
fragment, literary, 10–11, 44, 50, 66, 122–24, 131, 142–43, 145
Frankfurt School, the, 5, 24, 29
Franz Kafka: Eine Biographie seiner Jugend. See Wagenbach, Klaus
Franz Kafka: Geometrician of Metaphor. See Sussman, Henry
Franz Kafka: Pictures of a Life. See Wagenbach, Klaus
Freud, Sigmund, 21, 65, 77, 91, 103, 109, 125, 151, 155–56, 160; *The Interpretation of Dreams,* 21, 103, 151, 156

García Márquez, Gabriel, 5
genre, 68, 73, 82, 95
gift, the, 40, 154
Goodman, Paul, 28, 153, 160
Gray, Ronald, 25, 30, 152, 154, 161
"Great Wall of China, The." *See* Kafka, Franz
Greenberg, Martin, 28, 153, 161
Gross, Ruth V., 31, 154, 161
Guattari, Felix, 27, 152, 160
guilt, 36–37, 39–40, 42, 50, 76, 81, 93, 96, 103, 114, 128, 147

Hall, Calvin S., and Richard E. Lind, 152, 161
Hamlet, 77

Hartmann, Heinz, 26
Hayman, Ronald, 5, 30, 151, 161
Heidegger, Martin, 17
Hiebel, Hans Helmut, 29, 153, 161
Histoire de l'érotisme. See Bataille, Georges
Hoffmann, E. T. A., 75
Hofmannsthal, Hugo von, 27
homoeroticism, 59, 69, 96, 109–11
Hughes, Kenneth, 30, 154, 161
humor, 40–41, 70, 88–91, 97, 100, 108, 123, 150
"Hunger Artist, A." *See* Kafka, Franz
Huxley, Aldous: *Brave New World,* 15

image, 9, 11, 54, 60, 94, 123, 129–31
In Remembrance of Things Past. See Proust, Marcel
indifference, 60, 94, 114, 118–19, 143, 150
interpretation, 11, 15, 18–31, 78, 84, 96–99, 111–12, 118, 121–24, 129, 131–34, 139–44
Interpretation of Dreams, The. See Freud, Sigmund
"Investigations of a Dog, The." *See* Kafka, Franz
irony, 16, 23, 97, 100, 130, 143, 147, 150
isolation. *See* alienation

Janouch, Gustav, 30, 154, 161
Jayne, Richard, vii, 22, 162
Jesenska–Pollak, Milena, xi–xii
Jews and Judaism, 7–9, 13, 25, 44, 90, 92
"Josephine the Singer, or the Mouse Folk." *See* Kafka, Franz
Joyce, James, 4, 19, 30, 80, 97, 110; *Finnegans Wake,* 19; *Portrait of the Artist as a Young Man,* 80; *Ulysses,* 80
"Judgment, The." *See* Kafka, Franz

Kafka, Franz. *See also* Franz Kafka

WORKS
Amerika, 11, 71, 102, 123
"Bucket Rider, The," 6
"Burrow, The," xii
"Cares of a Family Man, The,"
36, 40, 43–45
Castle, The, xii, 11, 28, 35, 37,
60, 64, 70, 100, 103, 123
"Children on a Country Road,"
64
Complete Stories, The, 36, 151,
158
"Country Doctor, A," 149
"Crossbreed, A [A Sport],"
40–43, 144
"Description of a Struggle," 13,
146, 156
Diaries 1914–23, 6–7, 59, 155,
158
"First Sorrow," 48, 50–55, 57,
79, 141
"Great Wall of China, The," 10,
28, 124, 131
"Hunger Artist, A," xii–xiii, 10,
36, 50–51, 55–60, 121
"Investigations of a Dog, The,"
xii
"Josephine the Singer, or the
Mouse Folk," xii, 6
"Judgment, The," x, 13, 26, 36,
45–50, 55, 57, 59–60, 67, 103
"Knock at the Manor Gate, The,"
36–40, 50
Letter to His Father, 11, 151
Letters to Felice, 30
"Meditation" (*Betrachtung*), x
"Metamorphosis, The," x, 10, 15,
26, 36, 70, 103, 107, 118
"Parable of the Doorkeeper,
The," 5, 19, 28, 35, 65–66,
70–71, 73, 97, 107, 112, 114,
118, 122–23, 129, 137–45

"Penal Colony, In the," xi, 28, 64
"Stoker, The" (first chapter of
Amerika), x
Kafka, Gabriele (Elli), ix, xii, 39
Kafka, Georg, 39
Kafka, Heinrich, ix
Kafka, Hermann, ix, 11, 50, 54,
123, 148
Kafka, Julie (Löwy), ix, 148
Kafka, Ottilie (Ottla), ix, xi–xii,
39
Kafka, Valerie (Valli), ix, 39
Kant, Immanuel, 75–77, 155; *The
Critique of Pure Reason*,
75–76, 155
Karst, Roman, vii
Kernberg, Otto, 26, 61
Klein, Melanie, 26
Kierkegaard, Søoren, 107
Kleist, Heinrich von, 75
Klopstock, Robert, xii
"Knock at the Manor Gate, The."
See Kafka, Franz
Koelb, Clayton, 30, 153, 162
Kohut, Heinz, 26, 61, 152, 156,
162; *The Analysis of the Self*,
152; *The Restoration of the
Self*, 26, 152, 162
Kuna, Franz, 27, 31, 153, 162

Law, the, 38–39, 49, 53–54, 56,
65–67, 71, 75–77, 79, 81,
97–101, 105, 109, 111,
122–26, 132–34, 137,
140–44, 150, 156
Law of the Ordinary, 79, 88–89
legacy, 13, 37, 40, 42–45, 48, 62,
76, 96, 112
Letter to His Father. See Kafka,
Franz
Letters to Felice. See Kafka, Franz
Lévi–Strauss, Claude, 29
logic, 3, 9–10, 15, 19, 39, 41–42,
44, 53, 73, 75–77, 101,

Index

122–23, 131–32, 134,
141–44, 150
Löwy, Alfred, 6, 64
Löwy, Richard, ix
Löwy, Rudolf, 64
Löwy, Siegfried, 8, 64
Löwy, Yitzak, x–xi

Mahler, Margaret, 26
Man Without Qualities, The. See
Musil, Robert
martyr, the, 11, 13, 28, 35, 37, 40,
50, 56, 58, 60, 80, 112, 147,
150
Mauss, Marcel, 154
"Meditation" (*Betrachtung*). *See*
Kafka, Franz
Melville, Herman, 72, 115
"Metamorphosis, The." *See* Kafka,
Franz
metaphor, 9–11, 29
metonymy, 91
misogyny, 59, 69–70, 106–107
Moholy–Nagy, Laszlo, 44
Murray, Jack, 27, 153, 162
Musil, Robert, 4, 61; *The Man
Without Qualities*, 4
Mykyta, Larysa, 152

Nägele, Rainer, 29
narcissism, 113
narrative unreliability, 40, 42, 46,
48–55, 58, 65, 89, 113, 116,
144, 147
negation, or negativity, 19, 36, 56,
58, 122, 132, 138
Neider, Charles, 28, 162
1984. See Orwell, George
nouveau roman, the, 24

Odradek, 43–44, 56, 61
Oedipus, or the oedipal, 17, 25, 76
Olsen, Regine, 107
Onetti, Juan Carlos, 27

Orwell, George: *1984*, 15
"ostensible acquittal," 120, 126–27
Ott, Ulrich, 30, 154

"Parable of the Doorkeeper, The."
See Kafka, Franz
parables, 22, 28, 36, 39–40, 42, 54,
77, 139–44
paradoxes, 9, 16, 23, 56, 75–77,
113, 118, 121–22, 131,
141–44, 150
Pasley, Malcolm, 30, 154
patrimony, see legacy
"Penal Colony, In the." *See* Kafka,
Franz
personality disorders, 65
phenomenology, 17
philosophy, 16–17, 24, 27, 75–76, 78
Picasso, Pablo, 43
Poe, Edgar Allan, 115
Politzer, Heinz, 23, 29, 152, 156,
163
Pollak, Oskar, ix
Portrait of the Artist as a Young Man.
See Joyce, James
"postponement," 120, 126–27, 131
Pound, Ezra, 4, 97
proliferation, 11, 59–60, 71, 91, 98,
123, 128, 134, 139–41, 143,
146
Proust, Marcel, 4, 64, 97, 110; *In
Remembrance of Things Past*, 4
psychoanalysis, 21–22, 25–27, 77,
137. *See also* critical approaches to *The Trial*, psychoanalytical
psychology, 17, 20–21, 25, 37,
61–62, 72, 85, 95–96, 112,
135–37, 143, 147–48, 150

representation, 11, 29–30, 43,
124–26, 129–31, 135, 139–44
Restoration of the Self, The. See
Kohut, Heinz

Rey, Jean-Michel, 30, 153, 163
Robbins, Jill, 28, 153n, 163
Robert, Marthe, 25, 163
Rochefort, Robert, 28, 163
Rolleston, James, 25, 31, 68, 152, 154, 163
Ronell, Avital, 29
Rowohlt, Ernst, x

Sacher-Masoch, Leopold, 27
sadomasochism, 69, 102, 108
"Sarrazine." *See* Balzac, Honoré de
Schlegel, Friedrich, 147, 157
Schneider, Romy, 70
Schoeps, Hans-Joachim, 36
Schorske, Carl E.:*Fin de Siècle Vienna: Politics and Culture*, 7, 163
Schulz, Bruno, 5
science fiction, 15
semiology, 37, 63–64, 75, 78, 84–85, 130–33
sexuality, 11, 15, 20, 59, 69–70, 81–84, 99, 102–111, 139–40
shame, 16, 35, 50, 65, 76, 80, 92, 105, 113, 121, 147
Sokel, Walter, 23, 25, 29, 152, 164
son, the, 11, 13, 28, 37–42, 44–51, 56, 60, 75, 94, 96, 101, 109, 119, 123, 129, 147
Space of Literature, The. See Blanchot, Maurice
spatio-temporal incoherence, 3, 5, 66, 91, 98, 146–47, 150
Spilka, Mark, 27, 152, 164
splitting, 54–56, 109–10, 116, 118, 120, 134, 141–42
Stein, Gertrude, 4, 97, 110
Stein, J. P., 31, 154, 164
Stirmer, Max, 27
"Stoker, The" (first chapter of *Amerika*). *See* Kafka, Franz
Stranger, The. See Camus, Albert

structuralism, 20, 29. *See also* critical approaches to *The Trial*, structuralist
subject-conditions, twentieth-century, 61–62
Sullivan, Harry Stack, 26
superimposition, 61
supplantation, 19, 132, 139–40, 143
Sussman, Henry, 29, 151, 153, 155, 157, 164; *Afterimages of Modernity*, 153, 157, 164; *Franz Kafka: Geometrician of Metaphor*, 29, 151, 164
synecdoche, 97
S/Z. See Barthes, Roland

technology, 7–9, 71
textuality, 71, 134, 141–43
theatricality, 25, 38–39, 68, 73, 81–82, 93, 95, 144, 148
theology, 92. *See also* critical approaches to *The Trial*, theological
Thorlby, Anthony, 25, 152, 164
Tolstoy, Leo, 27
tragedy, 38–39, 54, 65, 80, 95, 97
transcendental, the, 75, 77
Trial, The. See Kafka, Franz. *See also* critical approaches to *The Trial*; women in Kafka's fiction and *The Trial*; Welles, Orson

Udoff, Alan, 29, 164
Ulysses. See Joyce, James
uncanny, the, 20, 41, 72, 91, 98, 100, 112, 125–26, 129, 148
unconscious, the, 21
uniforms. *See* clothing
Unseld, Joachim, 154, 164

Wagenbach, Klaus, 8, 21, 30, 88, 151, 164; *Franz Kafka: Eine*

Index

Biographie seiner Jugend, 30, 164; *Franz Kafka: Pictures of a Life*, 8, 151, 164
Welles, Orson: *The Trial*, 70
Wilson, Edmund, 24, 152
Winnicott, D. W., 26
withdrawal. *See* alienation
Wittgenstein, Ludwig, 17, 30
Wohryzek, Julie, xi
Wolff, Kurt, x

women in Kafka's fiction and *The Trial*, 21–22, 59, 66, 72–73, 79, 81, 93, 121, 139, 146. *See also* critical approaches to *The Trial*, feminist
Woolf, Virginia, 4
World War I, 4–7
wound, narcissistic, 113

Zionism, 7

The Author

Henry Sussman was born in 1947 in Philadelphia, attended Temple and Brandeis Universities, and earned his Ph.D. in comparative literature from Johns Hopkins University. He has published four other books: *Afterimages of Modernity* (Baltimore: Johns Hopkins University Press, 1990), *High Resolution: Critical Theory and the Problem of Literacy* (New York: Oxford University Press, 1989), *The Hegelian Aftermath: Readings in Hegel, Kierkegaard, Freud, Proust, and James* (Baltimore: Johns Hopkins University Press, 1982), and *Franz Kafka: Geometrician of Metaphor* (Madison, Wis.: Coda Press, 1979). *Psyche and Text: The Sublime and the Grandiose in Literature, Psychopathology, and Culture* is forthcoming from SUNY Press. Between 1981 and 1985 he served as interim and associate dean of arts and letters, SUNY/Buffalo. Since 1986 he has served as director of comparative literature at the same university. He has received NEH and Rockefeller Humanities Fellowships. He has twice been a Fellow at the Camargo Foundation, Cassis, France. He belongs to the Johns Hopkins Society of Scholars.